THE CAMBRIDGE BIBLE COMMENTARY

NEW ENGLISH

GENERAL ED

P. R. ACKROYD, A. R. C. LE

GENESIS 1–11

GENESIS 1–11

COMMENTARY BY
ROBERT DAVIDSON
*Professor of Old Testament Language and Literature,
University of Glasgow*

CAMBRIDGE
AT THE UNIVERSITY PRESS
1973

Published by the Syndics of the Cambridge University Press
Bentley House, 200 Euston Road, London NW1 2DB
American Branch: 32 East 57th Street, New York, N.Y.10022

© Cambridge University Press 1973

Library of Congress Catalogue Card Number: 72–93675

ISBNS:
0 521 08618 3 hard covers
0 521 09760 6 paperback

Printed in Great Britain
at the University Printing House, Cambridge
(Brooke Crutchley, University Printer)

GENERAL EDITORS' PREFACE

The aim of this series is to provide the text of the New English Bible closely linked to a commentary in which the results of modern scholarship are made available to the general reader. Teachers and young people have been especially kept in mind. The commentators have been asked to assume no specialized theological knowledge, and no knowledge of Greek and Hebrew. Bare references to other literature and multiple references to other parts of the Bible have been avoided. Actual quotations have been given as often as possible.

The completion of the New Testament part of the series in 1967 provides a basis upon which the production of the much larger Old Testament and Apocrypha series can be undertaken. The welcome accorded to the series has been an encouragement to the editors to follow the same general pattern, and an attempt has been made to take account of criticisms which have been offered. One necessary change is the inclusion of the translators' footnotes since in the Old Testament these are more extensive, and essential for the understanding of the text.

Within the severe limits imposed by the size and scope of the series, each commentator will attempt to set out the main findings of recent biblical scholarship and to describe the historical background to the text. The main theological issues will also be critically discussed.

Much attention has been given to the form of the volumes. The aim is to produce books each of which will be read consecutively from first to last page. The introductory material leads naturally into the text, which itself leads into the alternating sections of the commentary.

The series is accompanied by three volumes of a more general character. *Understanding the Old Testament* sets out to provide the larger historical and archaeological background, to say something about the life and thought of the people of the Old Testament, and to answer the question 'Why should we study the Old Testament?'. *The Making of the Old Testament* is concerned with the formation of the books of the Old Testament and Apocrypha in the context of the ancient near eastern world, and with the ways in which these books have come down to us in the life of the Jewish and Christian communities. *Old Testament Illustrations* contains maps, diagrams and photographs with an explanatory text. These three volumes are designed to provide material helpful to the understanding of the individual books and their commentaries, but they are also prepared so as to be of use quite independently.

P. R. A.
A. R. C. L.
J. W. P.

CONTENTS

The footnotes to the N.E.B. text   *page* ix

✻   ✻   ✻   ✻   ✻   ✻   ✻   ✻   ✻   ✻   ✻   ✻   ✻

Behind the book   1

The sources of the book   2

The purpose of Genesis 1–11   8

The meaning of myth   9

✻   ✻   ✻   ✻   ✻   ✻   ✻   ✻   ✻   ✻   ✻   ✻   ✻

The creation of the world   12

The beginnings of history   28

The flood and the tower of Babel   64

✻   ✻   ✻   ✻   ✻   ✻   ✻   ✻   ✻   ✻   ✻   ✻   ✻

A NOTE ON FURTHER READING   113

INDEX   115

EDITOR'S PREFACE

I wish gratefully to acknowledge the help I have received in the preparation of this commentary from the general editors, Professor P. R. Ackroyd, Professor A. R. C. Leaney and the Rev. J. W. Packer. Their incisive comments have helped at many points to clarify my own thinking; their eagle eyes have rid the manuscript of many errors. Those which remain are my responsibility. I am also indebted to Mrs Carol Weimar for typing assistance and to Miss Moyra McCallum for proof reading and the preparation of the index. A commentator on Genesis is fortunate in the material on which he can draw. My indebtedness to previous commentators will be evident to all who have any acquaintance with the subject. Some of the books which have been most helpful to me will be found listed at the end of this volume.

R. D.

THE FOOTNOTES TO THE
N.E.B. TEXT

The footnotes to the N.E.B. text are designed to help the reader either to understand particular points of detail – the meaning of a name, the presence of a play upon words – or to give information about the actual text. Where the Hebrew text appears to be erroneous, or there is doubt about its precise meaning, it may be necessary to turn to manuscripts which offer a different wording, or to ancient translations of the text which may suggest a better reading, or to offer a new explanation based upon conjecture. In such cases, the footnotes supply very briefly an indication of the evidence, and whether the solution proposed is one that is regarded as possible or as probable. Various abbreviations are used in the footnotes.

(1) Some abbreviations are simply of terms used in explaining a point: *ch(s)*., chapter(s); *cp*., compare; *lit*., literally; *mng*., meaning; *MS(S)*., manuscript(s), i.e. Hebrew manuscript(s), unless otherwise stated; *om*., omit(s); *or*, indicating an alternative interpretation; *poss*., possible; *prob*., probable; *rdg*., reading; *Vs(s)*., Version(s).

(2) Other abbreviations indicate sources of information from which better interpretations or readings may be obtained.

Aq. Aquila, a Greek translator of the Old Testament (perhaps about A.D. 130) characterized by great literalness.

Aram. Aramaic – may refer to the text in this language (used in parts of Ezra and Daniel), or to the meaning of an Aramaic word. Aramaic belongs to the same language family as Hebrew, and is known from about 1000 B.C. over a wide area of the Middle East, including Palestine.

Heb. Hebrew – may refer to the Hebrew text or may indicate the literal meaning of the Hebrew word.

Josephus Flavius Josephus (A.D. 37/8–about 100), author of the *Jewish Antiquities*, a survey of the whole history of his people, directed partly at least to a non-Jewish audience, and of various other works, notably one on the *Jewish War* (that of A.D. 66–73) and a defence of Judaism (*Against Apion*).

Luc. Sept. Lucian's recension of the Septuagint, an important edition made in Antioch in Syria about the end of the third century A.D.

Pesh. Peshitta or Peshitto, the Syriac version of the Old Testament.

Syriac is the name given chiefly to a form of Eastern Aramaic used by the Christian community. The translation varies in quality, and is at many points influenced by the Septuagint or the Targums.

Sam.   Samaritan Pentateuch – the form of the first five books of the Old Testament as used by the Samaritan community. It is written in Hebrew in a special form of the Old Hebrew script, and preserves an important form of the text, somewhat influenced by Samaritan ideas.

Scroll(s)   Scroll(s), commonly called the Dead Sea Scrolls, found at or near Qumran from 1947 onwards. These important manuscripts shed light on the state of the Hebrew text as it was developing in the last centuries B.C. and the first century A.D.

Sept.   Septuagint (meaning 'seventy'); often abbreviated as the Roman numeral (LXX), the name given to the main Greek version of the Old Testament. According to tradition, the Pentateuch was translated in Egypt in the third century B.C. by 70 (or 72) translators, six from each tribe, but the precise nature of its origin and development is not fully known. It was intended to provide Greek-speaking Jews with a convenient translation. Subsequently it came to be much revered by the Christian community.

Symm.   Symmachus, another Greek translator of the Old Testament (beginning of the third century A.D.), who tried to combine literalness with good style. Both Lucian and Jerome viewed his version with favour.

Targ.   Targum, a name given to various Aramaic versions of the Old Testament, produced over a long period and eventually standardized, for the use of Aramaic-speaking Jews.

Theod.   Theodotion, the author of a revision of the Septuagint (probably second century A.D.), very dependent on the Hebrew text.

Vulg.   Vulgate, the most important Latin version of the Old Testament, produced by Jerome about A.D. 400, and the text most used throughout the Middle Ages in western Christianity.

[. . .]   In the text itself square brackets are used to indicate probably late additions to the Hebrew text.

(Fuller discussion of a number of these points may be found in *The Making of the Old Testament* in this series.)

GENESIS

✳   ✳   ✳   ✳   ✳   ✳   ✳   ✳   ✳   ✳   ✳   ✳   ✳

BEHIND THE BOOK

We are accustomed to think of a book as a document written by one person. The author's name appears on the cover; the date and place of publication are given. Often in a 'Foreword' the author briefly explains for the benefit of his readers the purpose of the book. To understand Genesis, and many other books in the Old Testament, we have to think our way into a very different world.

Writing was known and used from an early age in Israel and in the wider world of the Ancient Near East. Religious texts, letters, political treaties survive in written form from a period before Israel as a nation ever existed. Writing, however, was a specialized skill, the possession of the few. It was neither the only, nor the most important way of preserving and handing on information. Many of the traditions of a people, their early tribal or national history, the stories and legends about their ancestors, were handed down *orally*, by word of mouth, from father to son, on the lips of tribal bards and poets. Much of the material now in the book of Genesis must have begun life in this way. Such traditions would have a generally accepted outline and content long before they were ever transferred into writing. Think of how unchangeable certain well-known stories become in the mind of a young child before ever the child can read or write. Even after such traditions did exist in writing, for most people they would continue, living within the community, in oral form.

But when and why were such traditions first committed to writing? There is good reason to believe that, as far as Israel was concerned, the answer lies in the foundation and establishment of the united Hebrew kingdom under David and Solomon in the tenth century B.C. Jerusalem then became the political and religious capital of a people who were riding on the crest of military success and economic growth. Just as England in the reign of Queen Elizabeth I produced great writers who reflect the confidence and vigour of the age, so in Israel of the tenth century B.C. the new national self-consciousness found an outlet in writers who recorded the events of the day in narratives such as those now found in 2 Samuel 9 – I Kings 2, and gave literary form to the traditions of the past. Contemporary confidence and hopefulness for the future drew strength from the recording of a past in which the purposive hand of God was seen at work, from the beginning. It has also been argued that the written record did not really come into its own until some four centuries later when Jerusalem was overrun by the Babylonians. The last remnant of the once powerful Hebrew kingdom had finally collapsed. With the breakdown of community life the continuing stream of oral tradition was in danger of disappearing. The need for written preservation of the nation's past thus became acute. Whenever it happened – and both periods may have made their contribution to the book of Genesis – no one was concerned to preserve the names of the earliest Hebrew historical writers.

THE SOURCES OF THE BOOK

Traditionally in Jewish circles Genesis is called *Bereshith*, 'In the beginning'. This follows the common practice of designating a book by its opening word or phrase. The title 'Genesis' comes from the Septuagint (LXX), the Greek translation of the Old Testament. Further information about the Septuagint will be found in 'The footnotes to the N.E.B. text', see p. xii. In Greek *genesis* means 'origin', 'beginning', or 'creation'. *Bereshith* is the first of five books called in ancient tradition 'the (five) books of Moses'. These five books, Genesis, Exodus, Leviticus, Numbers, Deuteronomy – often referred to in modern discussion as the Pentateuch (the five books) – constitute for the Jew *TORAH*, the most important part of the Old Testament. 'Law' is the conventional translation of *TORAH* but perhaps 'revelation' would be nearer the mark. *TORAH* means the instruction or teaching concerning God's purposes and demands which had been given to Israel, according to tradition, through Moses. It was early recognized that to attribute the whole of Genesis–Deuteronomy to Moses was impossible. The obituary notice of Moses in Deuteronomy 34 is an obvious case in point. But if not Moses, then who? Is it indeed possible to think of any one author as responsible for Genesis–Deuteronomy, or even for Genesis alone?

Three examples from Genesis will illustrate the problem.

(i) Anyone who reads from the beginning of Genesis must become aware that the character of the writing changes between verses 4 and 5 of chapter 2. The N.E.B. indicates this by putting a major division of the text at this point. The opening chapter is hymn-like, formal in structure, very carefully schematized. Certain key words and phrases occur again and again, e.g. 'God said . . . and so it was . . . Evening came and morning came'. The deliberate use of repetition is well illustrated in 1: 27: 'So God created man in his own image; in the image of God he created him; male and female he created them.' Throughout the chapter the language used to describe God is very restrained and dignified. From the words 'When the LORD God made earth and heaven', however, there is a marked difference. Here is narrative, simple yet remarkably vivid. Certain of the key words and phrases of chapter 1 have disappeared. Instead of 'created' we find 'formed' (2: 7). The language used to describe God is much more homely. He is like a potter forming man; he breathes into man's nostrils the breath of life (2: 7). He plants a garden (2: 8). He is heard 'walking in the garden at the time of the evening breeze' (3: 8). At precisely the point where such changes begin, a new name for God appears; he is now the LORD God.

(ii) Turn to the flood story in Genesis 6–8. Here again the story as it now lies before us is a curious patchwork of passages which use different divine names. In 6: 5–8; 7: 1–5 and 8: 20–2 it is the LORD; but elsewhere it is God, with the exception of 7: 16 where within one verse both God and the LORD appear. Furthermore, what the LORD says to Noah in 7: 1–5 is curiously like a repetition of what God says to Noah in 6: 9–22. Repetition is common enough in ancient narrative texts, but there also seem to be contradictions. In 6: 19 Noah is told by God to take with him into the ark living creatures of every kind, 'two of each kind, a male and a female'. In 7: 2, however, the LORD orders Noah to take with him into the ark 'seven pairs, male and female, of all beasts that are ritually clean', acceptable for use in sacrifice, 'and one pair, male and female, of all beasts that are not clean; also seven pairs, male and female, of every bird'. Again in 7: 4 the LORD warns Noah that he will send 'rain over the earth for forty days and forty nights', and this is described as happening in 7: 12. In 7: 24, however, God thinks of Noah 'when the waters had increased over the earth for a hundred and fifty days'.

(iii) Three times in Genesis a very similar story is told of how one of the patriarchs passes off his wife as his sister. Twice the narratives feature Abraham and his wife Sarah, once when they were in Egypt (12: 10–20), once when they were resident in Gerar under the jurisdiction of King Abimelech (20). The third narrative concerns Isaac and his wife Rebecca; again the third party involved is Abimelech, the Philistine king of Gerar (26: 1–11).

Differences in style and vocabulary, duplicate narratives, contradictions, different divine names – such things occur at point after point throughout the first five books of the Old Testament. How do we account for them?

4

As traditional stories, laws and customs, were handed down orally within the Hebrew community, they would naturally tend to reflect the interests of the groups in which they circulated. Thus basically the same story told in a community in the northern part of the country and in a community in the southern part of the country would, in its detail, have a northern or southern colouring. The sanctuary at Bethel would keep alive one set of stories linking the patriarchs with the Bethel sanctuary, while the priests at Hebron would have their own traditions linking these same patriarchs with Hebron. Similarly we would expect material which circulated in priestly circles as part of the continuing theological education of the priesthood to have a rather different character from the popular stories recounted by tribal bards. There are those who believe that the books of Genesis, Exodus, Leviticus and Numbers are, in their present form, the result of a gradual, centuries-long coalescing of such traditions from many different circles. The priestly editors, who gave final shape to the whole during the breakdown of the nation's life in the period of the Babylonian exile, preserved the character of the different traditions, and made little attempt to eliminate discrepancies between them.

Deuteronomy is now usually separated from the first four books of the Old Testament. It shares a common outlook and judgement on events with the succeeding historical narratives in Judges, 1 and 2 Samuel and 1 and 2 Kings, and is best considered in relationship with them. It seems likely, however, that in the composition of Genesis, Exodus, Leviticus and Numbers there was an intermediate stage at which the material existed in three independent, written sources, each with its own literary characteristics of vocabulary, style and interest. These sources may be represented by the symbols J, E and P. J, the earliest of these written sources, ninth or tenth century B.C., comes from Judah, in the South. It consistently refers to God as YHWH, four Hebrew consonants, traditionally but quite erroneously rendered into

English as *Jehovah*. Most English versions translate YHWH
as the *LORD*. *Yahweh* is probably as near as we can get to the
pronunciation of what for the Hebrews was the personal
name of their God, a name which became so sacred that the
custom grew up of not pronouncing it. When a Jew came to
the letters *YHWH* in the sacred text he substituted the word
Adonai ('my lord'). The form *Jehovah* arose through inserting
the vowels from *Adonai* into the consonants *YHWH*. J first
appears in the Genesis narrative at 2: 5. E, probably a century
later, comes from Israel (Ephraim) the northern part of the
divided Hebrew kingdom. From Genesis 15 onward it
provides a narrative parallel in many respects to J, although
it is not always easy to distinguish the two sources. It is
possible to regard E as a revision of J. The latest of the documents, P, possibly fifth century B.C., is a priestly source which
provides the framework within which the other two sources
find their place. The character and interests of P are well
exemplified by the hymn of creation in Genesis 1: 1 – 2: 4.

It must be admitted that this is a hypothesis. No one has
ever seen a document labelled J or E or P; but it is a hypothesis
which provides a reasonable explanation for the problems
which confront us when we study in detail the material in
Genesis–Numbers.

As outlined above the hypothesis is the logical outcome
of over two hundred years of intensive study of the Pentateuch, study which received its classical formulation in the
nineteenth century in the 'Documentary hypothesis'. Fuller
discussion of the sources and further information about this
hypothesis will be found in the introductory volume to this
series, *The Making of the Old Testament*, pp. 6off.

Two points about this hypothesis are worth stressing:

(i) The date assigned to a source does not decide the antiquity of the material within that source, nor is it a sure guide
to the religious value of that material. It is demonstrable, for
example, that P, the latest source, contains very old material,
particularly in its description of religious rites which tend to

be tenaciously conservative. Likewise the fact that J is held
to be the earliest source does not mean that it is the most
primitive or naïve in outlook. No one who carefully reads
the J story of the Garden in Genesis, chapters 2 and 3, should
be in any doubt that it is the work of one who is not only a
skilled literary artist but also a profound thinker.

(ii) J, E and P must not be thought of as free-lance authors.
As we have seen, they inherit, and are the servants of, their
people's religious and historical traditions. This does not mean
that they have no originality. Far from it. They reshape what
they inherit. They link together once independent traditions
in such a way that they take on new meaning. Genesis 6 is a
good example. It opens (verses 1-4) with the strange episode
of 'the sons of the gods' and 'the daughters of men'. Stories
of the gods having intercourse with mortal women are
common enough in religious mythology. Nor is it surprising
that such a story should be used to explain the existence on
earth of a race of giants, called in verse 4 'Nephilim'. As
such, this episode stands on its own, with its own meaning.
Yet J has deliberately changed the character of these verses.
He has done this by placing them as the prologue to the
story of the flood, and by linking them to the flood story by
his own commentary (6: 5-7) in which he stresses the depth
and dimension of that evil in the world which makes God's
judgement inevitable. He is thus inviting us to re-interpret
the story so that it becomes an illustration of the universality
of evil infecting not only the world of man but even celestial
beings.

Genesis preserves many of the old religious and historical
traditions of Israel. In the form in which they now lie before
us they have been reminted by some of Israel's greatest
thinkers; no less great because they are anonymous, known
to us only by the symbols J, E and P.

THE PURPOSE OF GENESIS I–II

The material in Genesis falls into two main sections:

(i) Chapters 1–11 which we may call 'the Prologue' and
(ii) Chapters 12–50, 'the patriarchal traditions'.

The two sections are linked by the list of the descendants of Shem (11: 10–26) and the list of the descendants of Terah (11: 27–32). It is only when we come to the story of Abraham in chapter 12 that we can claim with any certainty to be in touch with traditions which reflect something of the historical memory of the Hebrew people. In this volume we are concerned only with chapters 1–11. Chapters 12–50 will be dealt with in a second volume. How are we to approach chapters 1–11? It may be helpful to think of these chapters as the Prologue, not merely to the rest of the book of Genesis, but to much of the Old Testament and the faith to which it bears witness. As such these chapters fulfil the same function as the Prologue to a Shakespearean play. Two things are worth noting about such a Prologue.

(i) The Prologue is written after the drama is already known to the author. We cannot understand Genesis 1–11 aright unless we recognize that behind these chapters lie the traditions concerning the patriarchs, the miracle of deliverance from Egyptian slavery, the settlement in Canaan, the advent of the Hebrew state and much of the knowledge of God which came to men of faith in Israel through these events. Genesis 1–11 are the opening chapters in our present Old Testament, but they are the fruit of reflection upon much that is found elsewhere in the Old Testament.

(ii) The Prologue makes an appeal to the imagination. Shakespeare in the Prologue to Henry V thus invites the spectators to use their imagination.

'can this cockpit hold
The vasty fields of France? Or may we cram
Within this wooden 'O' the very casques

That did affright the air at Agincourt?
Think when we talk of horses, that you see them
Printing their proud hoofs i' the receiving earth.
For 'tis your thoughts that must now deck our kings,
Carry them here and there, jumping over times,
Turning the accomplishment of many years
Into an hour glass.'

So Genesis I-II makes an appeal to the imagination of faith to grasp that what was being played out on the narrow stage of Israel was of significance for all time and for all men. Within the history of one people, and that never a very important or significant people politically, there is revealed, claims this Prologue, the God who is the lord of all history, the source of all life. In Israel's encounter with God the truth about 'Everyman' is laid bare. The book of Genesis begins with the broad canvas of creation and narrows down to the particular history of one nation in its pilgrim forefather Abraham. Israel's religious experience was the reverse. It began with that one pilgrim and moved out in ever widening circles till it claimed universal significance. Genesis I-II is one of the ways in which this claim is made.

THE MEANING OF MYTH

The word 'myth' has been, and is, so frequently applied to some of the contents of Genesis I-II that it is as well, when discussing the nature of these chapters, to begin by explaining its meaning. Myth is a word which has been badly devalued in popular usage. We speak of something as 'mere myth' when we wish to indicate that it is wholly illusory or devoid of any truth. It should hardly need to be said that this is not what is meant when a scholar describes Genesis I-II as myth. More seriously, the word myth is being commonly used today to mean little more than religious language or the thought-world of the Bible. There are, however, two clearly definable usages of the word which may be helpful for our understanding of Genesis 1–11.

(i) In many different cultures we find what we may describe as 'story myths'. Such 'story myths' are not told for their entertainment value. They provide answers to questions people ask about life, about society and about the world in which they live. To the extent to which they give explanations, such 'story myths' are often described as 'aetiological', from the Greek word *aitia* meaning 'cause'. The questions answered may range all the way from questions about the deepest mysteries of life to questions about local tribal customs. One South African 'story myth', for example, answers the following questions. Why are men mortal? Why does the hare have a cleft lip? Why does the hare always seem to be running? Why does the moon have marks on its face? Why is hare's flesh taboo to the tribe?

Such 'story myths' appear in two forms. They may be traditional, popular stories handed down within the community from generation to generation, their ultimate origin lost in the mists of antiquity. But they may also be the conscious literary creation of a teacher whose concern is to help others to share his insights into the meaning of life. Plato's myth of the prisoners in the cave in Book VII of the Republic is a good example of this second type. When Glaucon, after listening to the story, says to Socrates, 'You are describing a strange scene and strange prisoners', Socrates replies 'They resemble us'.

Some of the material in Genesis 1–11 may be handled as 'story myths', e.g., the story of the Garden (2: 5 – 3: 24), the Flood (chapters 6–8), the Tower of Babel (11: 1–9). Such stories may draw on fantasy – this is probably true of the story of the Garden (see commentary pp. 32–3); or they may draw on fact. The Flood story uses the memory or knowledge of severe floodings in southern Mesopotamia; the Tower of Babel has as its background the soaring temple towers of Mesopotamia (see commentary pp. 105–7).

Whether drawing on fact or fantasy, such 'story myths' are the way in which the Hebrew writer invites us to share his God-given insights into the mystery of life. On this view, our primary concern in Genesis 2: 5 – 3: 24 is not with questions such as the possible geographical location of the Garden or the chronology of Adam. Adam is not the first man who lived at a particular place and time in human history; he is 'Everyman', the 'Everyman' in us. Similarly in Genesis 6–8 it is a waste of time to discuss the potential sea-worthiness of Noah's ark, and a waste of money to mount archaeological expeditions to recover fragments of the ark from Mount Ararat. The Flood is a story not of a past event, but of an ever present reality, the fact of evil in the world and the inevitable judgement of God upon such evil.

(ii) The world of the Ancient Near East, however, was familiar with myth of a rather different kind, myth as the spoken word which accompanied the performance of certain all-important religious rituals. Myth in this sense is the libretto of the community liturgy. It declares in word what the ritual is designed to ensure through action. Such myths are therefore closely related to the basic needs of man and the society in which he lives. They usually focus upon the beneficent and harmful forces in man's natural environment. But such forces are never spoken of as objects in myths; always they are personalized as gods and goddesses, mutually inter-related and often locked in conflict with one another. Thus the recurring conflict between fertility and drought, life and death, is celebrated in the fourteenth century B.C. mythological texts from Ugarit in North Syria as the struggle between *Baal*, the god of the fertilizing rain, and his arch-enemy *Mot*, death. In this context, a 'Creation myth' is widespread in the Ancient Near East, not primarily because man was intellectually curious about the origin of the world, but because such a myth answers a continuing need. What guarantee can man have of the continuing stability of the natural world and the society to which he belongs? Orderly life now exists only because in the beginning the forces of order triumphed over the powers of chaos. But chaos is ever threatening to break down the structures of life. Therefore from time to time, and most appropriately at such a turning point as the end or beginning of the year, the triumph of order over chaos is relived by the community in word (myth) and act (ritual).

Against the background of this understanding of reality let us examine the account of creation in Genesis 1: 1 – 2: 4.

*   *   *   *   *   *   *   *   *   *   *   *   *

The creation of the world

THE SOVEREIGNTY OF GOD

1 IN THE BEGINNING of creation, when God made heaven
2 and earth,*a* the earth was without form and void, with darkness over the face of the abyss, and a mighty wind
3 that swept*b* over the surface of the waters. God said,
4 'Let there be light', and there was light; and God saw that the light was good, and he separated light from
5 darkness. He called the light day, and the darkness night. So evening came, and morning came, the first day.

* There are three possible ways of translating the first three verses of this chapter:

(i) Verse 1 may be taken with the N.E.B. footnote, and most earlier English translations, as an independent statement: *In the beginning God created heaven and earth.*

(ii) With N.E.B., verse 1 may be taken as a temporal clause: *In the beginning of creation, when God made heaven and*

[*a*] *Or* In the beginning God created heaven and earth.
[*b*] *Or* and the spirit of God hovering.

earth. The first main statement then comes in verse 2: *the earth was without form and void.*

(iii) After verse 1, taken as a temporal clause, the whole of verse 2 may be regarded as a parenthesis describing primeval chaos: *the earth* being *without form . . . and a mighty wind sweeping over the surface of the waters.* The first main statement then comes in verse 3: *God said, 'Let there be light'.*

All three translations are linguistically possible. In favour of (ii) or (iii) is the parallel with the Mesopotamian Creation epic which begins with a temporal clause:

'When on high, heaven had not been named
Firm ground below had not been called by name'

and then proceeds, in an aside, to describe the primeval chaos of waters, before recounting the story of creation. In context, however, the translation given in the N.E.B. footnote seems preferable. This independent statement provides the formal, keynote introduction to the entire section. It speaks of a relationship between God and the world which clearly differentiates Genesis 1 from other creation myths in the Ancient Near East. The Mesopotamian creation myth is extant in its fullest form in a Babylonian version, recited on the fourth day of the Babylonian New Year Festival. In it *Marduk*, the Babylonian champion of the gods, crushes the powers of chaos led by the goddess *Tiamat*. His kingship is then acclaimed by the other gods and goddesses. It has been argued that Genesis 1: 1 – 2: 4 originated in a parallel Hebrew New Year Festival, known elsewhere in the Old Testament as the pilgrim-feast of Tabernacles, the seven days of creation corresponding to the seven days of the festival (Deut. 16: 13–15; Lev. 23: 39–45). It seems better to regard Genesis 1: 1 – 2: 4 as the Old Testament counterstatement to certain of the presuppositions in such a creation myth. The contrast has been described in terms of the 'exuberant and grotesque polytheism' of the Mesopotamian myth and the 'severe and dignified monotheism' of Genesis. Although true, this hardly penetrates to the basic difference. The polytheism of the Mesopotamian myth is not grotesque; it is but the inevitable consequence of thinking of religion in terms of the need of man to control the natural forces which shape his life. Most of the gods and goddesses of the Mesopotamian myth are personifications of different aspects of nature – *Apsu* and *Tiamat*, the two great seas, the primeval waters of chaos, *Anu*, the sky, *Ea*, the earth. Since there are conflicting forces in nature, some beneficent, some destructive, it is hardly surprising that creation emerges out of conflict among the gods. Genesis I strips creation of this mythological character. The entire conflict theme has disappeared. The God of the Genesis creation story is not one of the forces of nature, not even the supreme fertility god or Nature with a capital N. He stands over against the world as its sovereign creator, the source of everything in it, but not identifiable with it. He is wholly other, the transcendent God.

Although Genesis I: I – 2: 4 is usually assigned on literary grounds to the P source, it is difficult to believe that this doctrine of the relationship between God and the world is a late post-exilic discovery. From the time of the settlement in Canaan (late thirteenth century B.C.) the recurring temptation to the Hebrews was to provide themselves with a Comprehensive Religious Insurance Policy. They were careful to worship Yahweh, the god who had delivered them out of Egyptian enslavement, but just as careful also to worship the Canaanite gods and goddesses, notably *Baal*, the god of the fertilizing rain. As an agricultural community they needed the farmers' god. The prophet Hosea bitterly complained in the name of Yahweh:

> 'She (i.e. Israel) does not know that it is I who
>   gave her corn, new wine and oil,
> I who lavished upon her silver and gold which
>   they spent on the Baal.' (Hos. 2: 8.)

The only effective answer to the seductive power of Canaanite religion was a doctrine of creation which would link the Hebrew God with the world as the source of all its life. Genesis 1: 1 – 2: 4 is best interpreted as priestly teaching, presented in hymn-like form and designed to combat the challenge of Canaanite religion at a time when that religion was still a living threat to Hebrew faith. It finds its closest parallels in the Psalms, notably Pss. 8 and 106.

But Genesis 1: 1 – 2: 4 is not merely concerned to link God with the world of nature. In context, within the book of Genesis, this creation hymn marks the beginning of history. It points to the meaning and purpose behind all history, just as the seer of Revelation sees the fulfilment of all history in terms of a new heaven and a new earth (Rev. 21: 1). The chronology in Genesis 5 traces the story of the ancestors of the Hebrew people back to 'the day when God created man' (Gen. 5: 1).

1. *In the beginning of creation when God made:* one Hebrew word lies behind the *of creation* and *made* in this translation. This word *bārā* is used predominantly of God's activity in the Old Testament. It is found frequently in Isaiah 40–55 with reference to God's creation of the world (40: 26, 28; 45: 12) and to God's work in history, his active control over all that happens in history (45: 7, 8), his creation of Israel to be his servant people in the world (43: 1, 7, 15). Here the word points to the absolute and effortless sovereignty of the God who brings the ordered universe out of primeval chaos.

2. Certain phrases, which have their roots in Ancient Near Eastern creation mythology, now describe this primeval chaos: The earth was *without form and void*, an alliterative phrase in Hebrew (*tōhū wā bōhū*) which signifies a confused, unordered, formless chaos, with *darkness over the face of the abyss*. The general picture here is similar to the opening stanza of the Babylonian creation myth in which, before even the heavens or the earth were created, there existed primordial *Apsu* and *Tiamat*, dark, swirling waters. The Hebrew word for the *abyss* (*tehōm*) is thought by some scholars to be

linked linguistically with *Tiamat*. This is doubtful. Whereas in the Babylonian version *Tiamat* is an active goddess, giving birth to other gods and fiercely opposing the gods of order, the *abyss* is merely the passive background upon which the drama of creation is enacted. This is all the more interesting since other poetic passages in the Old Testament show that Hebrew literature was well aware of the theme of a mythological conflict between God and the powers of chaos symbolized by the abyss and the monsters associated with it (Isa. 51: 9–10; Ps. 74: 12–14). Here there is no conflict, only a *mighty wind* sweeping over the waters. This rendering of a phrase which may be literally rendered 'wind of God', assumes that 'of God' is used adjectivally in much the same way as English uses 'almighty'. This is certainly possible. In Genesis 30: 8 a phrase which could be rendered literally 'wrestlings of God' is translated, 'mighty wrestlings' (R.S.V.) and 'a fine trick' (N.E.B.). Yet it is difficult to see why 'god' should be used in this adjectival sense here when it occurs more than thirty times elsewhere in this creation hymn in its primary sense. It seems better to translate, with the N.E.B. footnote, *the spirit of God*. This phrase then describes not chaos but the creative power of God in action. Wind, a symbol of power, is used theologically in the Old Testament to refer to the dynamic activity and presence of God in the world – his Spirit. To this Spirit is attributed all that surpasses the ordinary ability of man; for example Joseph's gift of interpreting dreams (Gen. 41: 38), the outstanding craftsmanship of Bezalel (Exod. 31: 3), Samson's prodigious strength (Judg. 15: 14). This spirit of God is also regarded as the source of life:

> 'the spirit of God made me,
> and the breath of the Almighty gave me life'

cries Job (Job 33: 4). Thus over the dark, life-less waters of chaos, the life-giving spirit of God is *hovering* or soaring – the same word is used in Deut. 32: 11 of an eagle hovering above its young.

16

3–5. *the first day:* the darkness is shattered by *light*, not the light which comes from the heavenly bodies – they are created later, see verses 14–19 – but *light* sent by God to negate the darkness of chaos and thus make an ordered universe possible. Jeremiah speaks of the breakdown of the ordered life of society in his day in terms of a return to primeval chaos, a life-less landscape, the earth becoming once more 'without form and void', a world bereft of 'light' (Jer. 4: 23). The account of God's creative acts is set within a fixed pattern.

(*a*) Each of the six days of creation is introduced by *God said, 'Let . . .'* The fulfilment of what God said is then indicated by the brief phrase *so it was*, sometimes accompanied by, or replaced by, a longer statement (verses 3, 16, 21, 27). This emphasis upon God's word finding its immediate fulfilment underlines both the absolute sovereignty of God over all creation and the fact that the entire creation reflects God's purposes.

(*b*) After most of the acts of creation there is pronounced a verdict, *good*. This verdict is omitted after the 'vault' of heaven (verse 7) and 'man' (verse 27), but all creation is included under the retrospective verdict of verse 31 'and God saw all that he had made, and it was very good'. If Genesis I: I – 2: 4 refuses to equate the world, or anything in it, with God, it equally rejects the opposite error of regarding the created world as evil or in some sense the enemy of God. Old Testament writers are far from being blind to the grim reality of evil and tragedy in the world, but the creation hymn is typical in refusing to seek an answer for this fact of evil in some form of dualism. As we shall see, Genesis 3 offers a different kind of approach to this problem. There runs through the Old Testament a rich vein of rejoicing in a world created good by God (see Pss. 104 and 148). It is in the richness of this world, not in withdrawal from it that man is confronted by God.

(*c*) Each section ends with the refrain *Evening came and*

morning came, the . . . day. The order, *evening* followed by *morning*, may reflect the early Old Testament religious calendar, where the day begins at sunset (cp. Lev. 23: 32) or it may signify no more than the fact that, in the mind of the writer, after the creation of light the close of the first half of the day is marked by the coming of *evening*, the close of the second half by the dawning of the new light. The flexibility in the usage of the word *day* is well illustrated in verse 5. In its first occurrence it means day time as distinct from the darkness of night; in the closing refrain it means the whole twenty-four hour cycle embracing both evening and morning. Attempts to make it still more flexible, to mean different aeons or stages in the known evolution of the world, and thus reconcile Genesis 1 with modern scientific theory, are misguided. The appeal of Genesis 1 is to the imagination; it is poetic, a hymn written by faith for faith. It is not a scientific hypothesis, nor does it need to be reconciled with any such hypothesis. *

THE SECOND DAY

6 God said, 'Let there be a vault between the waters,
7 to separate water from water.' So God made the vault, and separated the water under the vault from the water
8 above it, and so it was; and God called the vault heaven. Evening came, and morning came, a second day.

* The waters are now divided by the *vault* (A.V., R.V., R.S.V., firmament) of heaven. In line with other ancient near eastern cosmologies, heaven is thought of as a solid, dome-like structure arching over the earth. The word *vault* in Hebrew can mean something beaten into shape like a piece of metal. Above this *vault* are gathered the waters which are to be the source of rain; below the *vault* are the waters which are to form seas, rivers and springs.

The statement *and so it was* would come most naturally at the end of verse 6, immediately after God's creative word, as in verse 9, and this is where the Septuagint places it. A certain roughness here and elsewhere has suggested to some scholars that the final form of the hymn is a blend of two once separate themes, in one of which the key motif was *God said* (cp. verses 3, 6, 9, 14, 20, 24) and in the other *God made* (verses 7, 16, 25). But we have no right to demand mechanical repetition from our author; within a more or less fixed formal structure he plays his own minor variations. In this case *and so it was* which normally follows *God said* has been placed after *God made*.

The absence of the verdict *good* at the end of this second day of creation – it is added by the Septuagint – may be explained by the fact that this creative act involving the *waters*, although begun on the second day, does not find its fulfilment until the waters under the vault are gathered together on the third day to make way for the appearance of dry land (verse 10). ✳

THE THIRD DAY

God said, 'Let the waters under heaven be gathered 9 into one place, so that dry land may appear'; and so it was. God called the dry land earth, and the gathering 10 of the waters he called seas; and God saw that it was good. Then God said, 'Let the earth produce fresh growth, 11 let there be on the earth plants bearing seed, fruit-trees bearing fruit each with seed according to its kind.' So it was; the earth yielded fresh growth, plants bearing seed 12 according to their kind and trees bearing fruit each with seed according to its kind; and God saw that it was good. Evening came, and morning came, a third day. 13

* From other Old Testament passages it is clear that the earth is regarded as a solid disk founded upon the subterranean waters which surface in the seas. In Ps. 24: 2 God is said to have

> 'founded it (the earth) upon the seas
> and planted it firm upon the waters beneath'
> (cp. Ps. 136: 6).

The security of the habitable earth, *the dry land*, depends upon God keeping in check the waters, both those above the vault of heaven and those gathered under the earth. The flood tradition in Gen. 7: 11 describes chaos overwhelming the earth in the following terms:

> 'all the springs of the great abyss broke through, the windows of the sky were opened'.

On this earth now appear the first signs of organic life, the *fresh growth* or greenness. This *fresh growth* is classified into two species:

(i) *plants*, such as cereals, directly producing self-propagating seed,

(ii) *fruit trees*, such as the olive and the citrus fruits, which carry their seed inside the fruit. *

THE FOURTH DAY

14 God said, 'Let there be lights in the vault of heaven to separate day from night, and let them serve as signs both
15 for festivals and for seasons and years. Let them also shine in the vault of heaven to give light on earth.' So it was;
16 God made the two great lights, the greater to govern the day and the lesser to govern the night; and with them
17 he made the stars. God put these lights in the vault of
18 heaven to give light on earth, to govern day and night,

and to separate light from darkness; and God saw that it
was good. Evening came, and morning came, a fourth 19
day.

* The picture drawn here of *lights*, the *greater* (the sun), the
lesser (the moon) and the *stars put* or set *in the vault of heaven* is
wholly remote from our space-age understanding of the
immensities of the universe. Yet it is not remote from our
questioning about the meaning of the universe and about the
forces which shape man's destiny. These verses are a deliberate
corrective to an important element in many ancient near
eastern, and other religions. They contain a strongly anti-
mythological flavour. Deliberately they avoid naming the
sun and the moon, both of which were widely worshipped.
The stars were likewise often thought to control man's
destiny. This entire astrological fatalism is here swept into the
religious wastepaper basket. *The greater* light, *the lesser* light
and *the stars* are but part of the created universe. They have no
independent existence or power. God has made them to be
lights or bearers of light; and to be *signs*, pointers marking
off (i) the *festivals*, the important occasions in the religious
calendar when God's sovereignty over all the forces in nature
and history was celebrated by his people, (ii) the passing of
time, the *seasons*, lit. days, and *years*. They also *govern*, give a
distinctive character to, *day and night*. *

THE FIFTH DAY

God said, 'Let the waters teem with countless living 20
creatures, and let birds fly above the earth across the
vault of heaven.' God then created the great sea-monsters 21
and all living creatures that move and swarm in the
waters, according to their kind, and every kind of bird;
and God saw that it was good. So he blessed them and 22

said, 'Be fruitful and increase, fill the waters of the seas;
23 and let the birds increase on land.' Evening came, and
morning came, a fifth day.

* Each part of the created universe is now populated with
appropriate *living creatures*: *the waters teem* with life, birds
of all kinds fly *across the vault of heaven.* The anti-mythological
strain in the hymn again becomes apparent by the way in
which specific mention is made of the *great sea-monsters.* The
sea-monster or dragon is one of the recurring mythological
personifications of chaos, and echoes of a struggle between
the God of Israel and such a chaos monster are found in
poetic and prophetic passages in the Old Testament:

'by thy power thou didst cleave the sea-monster in two
and break the sea-serpent's heads above the waters'
(Ps. 74: 13; cp. Isa. 51: 9).

Here the sea-monsters are no threat to God. They are as much
part of the finite structure of creation, as much under the
control and sovereignty of God as the birds which fly across
the vault of heaven. The coming of *living creatures* marks a
new and significant stage in the creation hymn. This is
indicated in two ways:

(i) by the reappearance of the word *created* (verse 21).
Apart from the opening statement of the chapter, everything
previously has been described either as being the direct result
of God's word or as having been 'made' by God.

(ii) by a blessing conferred by God upon these creatures.
The blessing is an important concept in the Old Testament.
It is never merely a formal matter of words; it implies the
transference from one person to another of power or vitality.
God here bestows upon *living* creatures the power to pass
on the life-gift they themselves have received from him,
Be fruitful and increase (verse 22). *

THE SIXTH DAY

God said, 'Let the earth bring forth living creatures, 24
according to their kind: cattle, reptiles, and wild animals,
all according to their kind.' So it was; God made wild 25
animals, cattle, and all reptiles, each according to its
kind; and he saw that it was good. Then God said, 26
'Let us make man in our image and likeness to rule the
fish in the sea, the birds of heaven, the cattle, all wild
animals on earth,[a] and all reptiles that crawl upon the
earth.' So God created man in his own image; in the 27
image of God he created him; male and female he created
them. God blessed them and said to them, 'Be fruitful 28
and increase, fill the earth and subdue it, rule over the
fish in the sea, the birds of heaven, and every living thing
that moves upon the earth.' God also said, 'I give you 29
all plants that bear seed everywhere on earth, and every
tree bearing fruit which yields seed: they shall be yours
for food. All green plants I give for food to the wild 30
animals, to all the birds of heaven, and to all reptiles on
earth, every living creature.' So it was; and God saw all 31
that he had made, and it was very good. Evening came,
and morning came, a sixth day.

٭ Two creative acts are assigned to this day. First, there
come the *living creatures* whose natural habitat is the earth.
They are listed in three categories, *wild animals*, *cattle* (domesti-
cated animals) and *reptiles*, all the creatures who *move* on the
surface of the ground. The focus of interest, however, is that
earth-bound creature who forms the apex of the creation
pyramid, *man*, Hebrew, *'ādām*, mankind, the human race.

[a] *So Pesh.; Heb.* all the earth.

What is said about man is distinctive in several ways.

(i) The form of the creation statement changes from the impersonal 'let something happen' to '*Let us make man*'. There has been much discussion as to why the plural *us* is used here of God. Early Christian writers naturally saw in it confirmation of the doctrine of the Trinity. This is a reading back into the Old Testament of much later doctrine and can hardly explain why the plural is so seldom used in this way in the Old Testament. More modern explanations have been sought along the lines of a royal plural or a plural of exhortation, but the Old Testament parallels cited are not very convincing. Elsewhere in the Old Testament the first person plural used with reference to God is only found in Gen. 3: 22; 11: 7 and Isa. 6: 8. In all these passages there is good reason to see in the background echoes of the mythological picture of the heavenly court with whom the supreme god takes council when important decisions have to be made: cp. Ps. 82: 1

'God takes his stand in the court of heaven
to deliver judgement among the gods themselves.'

Added solemnity and significance is thus given to what now takes place, the creation of man. The hymn, however, leaves us in no doubt that it is the one supreme God of Hebrew faith who created man. This is made clear by the succession of singular verbs in verse 27: *So God created . . . he created him . . . he created them*. From within the certainties of his own firmly monotheistic faith, the author of Genesis 1 does not hesitate to use for his own purposes traditional mythological material.

(ii) Not only is the word *create* used repeatedly with reference to man, but a phrase occurs which refers to man and to man alone: '*Let us make man in our image and likeness*'. These words have been called 'The Magna Carta of Humanity'; but what do they mean? Most frequently in the Old Testament *image* (Hebrew *tselem*) indicates some formal representation such as a statue or idol of a god (cp. Amos 5: 26; 2 Kings 11: 18), but it can also mean any copy or duplicate. *likeness* (Hebrew *demūt*) is a more general, abstract term indicating resemblance. It is doubtful, however, whether the meaning of such a compound phrase can be decided by any analysis of the individual words. Each age has tended to read into the phrase its own highest ideals about man. Thus to a Greek-speaking Jew in Alexandria of the first century it means 'immortality'; and to an early twentieth century commentator it is 'the gift of self-conscious reason'. Others have found in it reference to man's upright bodily form. Context is the safest guide to meaning. *image and likeness* are defined by what follows, *to rule the fish in the sea* ... (verse 26). The blessing given to man has the same peculiar content; not merely as in the case of other living creatures, *Be fruitful and increase, fill the earth* but also *subdue it, rule over the fish in the sea* ... (verse 28). Just as God is sovereign over all creation, including man, so man reflects this sovereignty. He has sovereignty delegated to him; he is given dominion over all other living creatures. Psalm 8, which echoes this creation hymn, describes man in the following terms:

> 'thou hast made him little less than a god,
> crowning him with glory and honour.
> Thou makest him master over all thy creatures;
> thou hast put everything under his feet' (Ps. 8: 5–6).

But there is another element implicit in this *image and likeness*. Precisely because man's sovereignty is a delegated sovereignty, he stands in a position of responsibility before God. He is capable of, and called to a personal relationship with God. He is addressed personally by God: '*I give you*', verse 29. The whole of the Old Testament is the story of the unfolding drama of this relationship as it was experienced in Israel, a relationship with potentialities for good and for evil.

(iii) *man* is created as a unity which includes both *male and female*. *So God created man* ...; *male and female he created them* (verse 27). Here again we may find a twofold emphasis. On the one hand, the creation hymn refuses to deify sex as in the fertility cults of Canaan with their sexual orgies, cults only too familiar to the Hebrews. In the worship of *Baal* and his consort *Asherah* resort to a temple prostitute, lit. 'a holy woman', was a 'holy' act of the deepest religious significance, cp. Hos. 4: 14. On the other hand, sex is firmly rooted within the good creative purposes of God, and the essential need of male and female for each other is underlined. Together they form the full unity which is human life. The Old Testament throughout is characterized by a very positive, wholesome evaluation of sex.

(iv) It is implied in verses 29–30 that within the original harmony of God's creation, man is vegetarian. Grain and fruit are his food; other living creatures feed on other types of vegetation. Contrast 9: 1–3 and the commentary p. 88. *

THE SEVENTH DAY

2 Thus heaven and earth were completed with all their
2 mighty throng. On the sixth*[a]* day God completed all the work he had been doing, and on the seventh day he
3 ceased from all his work. God blessed the seventh day and made it holy, because on that day he ceased from all the work he had set himself*[b]* to do.

4   This is the story of the making of heaven and earth when they were created.

* N.E.B. has rightly ignored the late, medieval chapter division. The hymn of creation continues down to *when they were created* (2: 4). According to the traditional verse division these words occur midway through verse 4; the creation hymn then runs from 1: 1 – 2: 4*a*, with the following narrative beginning at 2: 4*b*. N.E.B. has attempted to simplify this by abbreviating verse 4 and making what is traditionally the second half of verse 4 the beginning of verse 5.

[a] *So Sam.; Heb.* seventh. [b] set himself: *prob. rdg., cp. Sept.; Heb.* created.

26

The sixth day marks the completion of God's creative acts. The *mighty throng* (lit. company or army, A.V., R.V., R.S.V. 'host'), everything that together makes up the cosmos, has come into being. Since all is completed on the sixth day, the reading of the Hebrew text *on the* seventh *day* (2: 2) must either be changed, following the Samaritan and Septuagint texts, to *on the sixth day* (N.E.B.), or the verb translated *completed* must be rendered 'declared' *completed*, i.e. on the seventh day God declared all the work he had been doing completed. It is perhaps misleading to say that God 'rested' on the seventh day. N.E.B. legitimately translates the word traditionally rendered 'rested' as *ceased, he ceased from all his work* (2: 2; cp. 2: 3). All that he had intended was now complete. This seventh day is given a peculiar character; it is *holy*, set apart, differentiated from all other days which have been filled with creative activity; it belongs to God and God alone. The origin of sabbath is obscure. Parallels from other ancient near eastern cultures have been widely canvassed. But within the Hebrew community, sabbath, a word derived from the verb translated *ceased*, has a distinctive character as a weekly day of rest, that recurring point in time which serves to remind the community of the meaning of all time. In one form of the Decalogue, or Ten Commandments, that found in Exod. 20, the reason for the community keeping the seventh day of the week as a rest day, sabbath, is traced back to God's action at creation (Exod. 20: 8-11); in the other form of the Decalogue in Deut. 5, sabbath is linked with the deliverance of the people from enslavement in Egypt (Deut. 5: 12-15). Whether the reference is to creation or to deliverance from Egypt, sabbath is essentially a day on which the community joyfully remembers and celebrates the gracious, mighty acts of God. In later Jewish writings and in the Letter to the Hebrews chapter 4, sabbath becomes a symbol of the ultimate consummation of all God's gracious purposes for his people.

4. *This is the story of* (A.V., R.V., R.S.V. 'these are the

generations of' . . .): this phrase is usually used by the priestly editors as the heading to a family history and, as such, is translated by N.E.B. 'These are the descendants of . . .' (Gen. 10: 1; 11: 10, 27; cp. 5: 1; 6: 9). Here the phrase is used metaphorically as a postscript to the creation hymn, summarizing the hymn and at the same time acting as a link to the succeeding narrative.

In faith, God has been acknowledged as the lord of everything that exists; the essential goodness of all creation has been affirmed and a peculiar stamp has been placed upon man and the time spectrum within which he lives out his God-given life. The nature of man is to be further explored in the narrative section which begins at 2: 5. *

The beginnings of history

When we move from the creation hymn to Gen. 2: 5 we enter a very different world. In place of the studied, rhythmic prose and hymn-like structure we find a deceptively simple, vivid narrative. In Gen. 2: 5 – 3: 24, we are in touch with the J tradition, with someone who is both a considerable literary artist and a profound religious thinker.

Whatever this narrative may be, it is impossible to describe it as historical in any of the usual senses of that word. To this extent the N.E.B. heading *The beginnings of history* is misleading. The characters in this story do not have personal names. As N.E.B. has rightly seen, Heb. *'ādām*, traditionally rendered Adam, should be translated simply *man* or *the man*. When the woman in the story is named she is called *ḥawwāh*, traditionally rendered Eve, but probably related to the Hebrew word for life (see p. 47). This is the story of 'Everyman'. The trees in the garden are not ordinary trees, but magical trees. The garden has strange creatures in it, a talking serpent (3: 1ff) and a guard of cherubim (3: 24). The whole purpose of the narrative is not to describe what once happened but to explain certain puzzling features of life and human experience known to the narrator. We are in the realm of story myth (see pp. 10–11). Not only is this story myth, but many features in it point to Mesopotamian traditions in the background. The 'tree of life' (2: 9; 3: 22) recalls the central motif of more than one Mesopotamian myth, man's search for that elusive immortality which is the prerogative of the gods. In the Epic of Gilgamesh (see pp. 64–7) the hero is given a plant whose name is 'man becomes young in old age', a plant which is later stolen from him by a serpent. The garden is described as being 'away to the east' (2: 8), and when a more precise geographical location is indicated in 2: 10–14, amid much that is enigmatic, two of the four rivers mentioned are the Tigris and the Euphrates.

But are we dealing with one story? Many duplications and apparent inconsistencies have led scholars to posit at least two independent strands out of which the present narrative has been woven. There seem to be two accounts of the placing of man in Eden (2: 8 and 2: 15), two accounts of the clothing of man (3: 7 and 3: 21). Above all there is the strange phenomenon of the two trees 'the tree of life' (2: 9; 3: 22) and 'the tree of the knowledge of good and evil' (2: 9, 17). Elsewhere there are references to 'the tree' (3: 3, 6). There has, however, been little agreement as to how the narrative ought to be divided. In terms of literary style, psychological insight and religious teaching the narrative as it lies before us has to be read as a unity. At most the writer seems to have drawn on different mythological traditions and woven them together into his own religious tapestry to illustrate the enigma of man.

THE MAKING OF MAN

When the LORD God made earth and heaven, there was 5 neither shrub nor plant growing wild upon the earth,

because the LORD God had sent no rain on the earth; nor
6 was there any man to till the ground. A flood*a* used to
rise out of the earth and water all the surface of the
7 ground. Then the LORD God formed a man*b* from the
dust of the ground*c* and breathed into his nostrils the
breath of life. Thus the man became a living creature.

✷ 5–6. Like the Babylonian creation epic this narrative
begins with a temporal clause, *When* (lit. on the day that) *the
LORD God.* The J tradition normally refers to God simply as
the LORD, Heb. YHWH (see p. 6). Within the Pentateuch
the phrase *the LORD God* is found only in this narrative in
Gen. 2: 5 – 3: 24 and once in Exod. 9: 30. The reason for its
usage here is not clear. It may reflect different traditions upon
which the writer has drawn or it may be the way in which the
final editors of Genesis draw our attention to the fact that the
God of Gen. 1 is the same as the LORD of Gen. 2: 5 ff.

The picture of creation here is very different from that of
Gen. 1 and the Babylonian creation epic. Instead of watery
chaos there is an arid, plantless, uninhabited wilderness. There
was no fertilizing rain, but periodically a *flood used to rise
out of the earth* (verse 6). The word translated *flood*, Heb.
'*ēd*, occurs only here and in Job 36: 27 where the N.E.B.
translates 'mist'. Both here and in the Job passage it is probably best, following Akkadian usage, to take the word to
refer to the subterranean waters which welled up from under
the earth before there was any rain moisture. Whatever its
precise details this picture is sketched merely by way of
background to the making of man.

7. *formed:* this word most frequently describes the activity
of a potter in the Old Testament. There is an Egyptian parallel
where the god Khnum fashions mankind on a potter's wheel.
a man from the dust of the ground: the Hebrew contains a

[a] *Or* mist.   [b] *Heb.* adam.
[c] *Heb.* adamah.

deliberate play on the similarity in sound between *'ādām* (man) and *'adāmāh* (ground). We get something of the same flavour in English if we translate, God formed 'an earthling from the dust of the earth'. Thus having shaped an inanimate statue God breathes into it the *breath of life* and man becomes a *living creature*. The A.V. 'living soul' is wholly misleading if it suggests that man now receives an immortal soul to dwell within his material body. Hebrew *nepesh* does not mean soul in the sense of the spiritual part of man; rather it means life, vitality, the total living personality. In Gen. 1: 24, 30 the same phrase refers to the living creature(s) of the animal world. The oneness of man with the rest of creation is being stressed. According to Gen. 2: 19 wild animals and birds are also formed out of the ground (*'adāmāh*) and in Gen. 7: 22 *the breath of life* belongs to all living creatures, birds, cattle, animals and reptiles as well as to man. With all other living creatures man experiences the frailty and transitoriness of life since this *breath of life*, given by God, may be withdrawn by God at any time. Both man and beast 'draw the same breath . . . all come from the dust, and to the dust all return' (Eccles. 3: 19; cp. Pss. 103: 14–16; 104: 29). The intensely personal way, however, in which God *breathed into his nostrils the breath of life* is J's way of indicating that peculiar relationship between God and man which the creation hymn described in terms of 'image' and 'likeness'. ✳

THE GARDEN OF EDEN

Then the LORD God planted a garden in Eden away to 8 the east, and there he put the man whom he had formed. The LORD God made trees spring from the ground, all 9 trees pleasant to look at and good for food; and in the middle of the garden he set the tree of life and the tree of the knowledge of good and evil.

There was a river flowing from Eden to water the 10

garden, and when it left the garden it branched into four

11 streams. The name of the first is Pishon; that is the river which encircles all the land of Havilah, where the gold[a]

12 is. The gold[a] of that land is good; bdellium[b] and corne-

13 lians are also to be found there. The name of the second river is Gihon; this is the one which encircles all the land

14 of Cush. The name of the third is Tigris; this is the river which runs east of Asshur. The fourth river is the Euphrates.

15 The LORD God took the man and put him in the

16 garden of Eden to till it and care for it. He told the man, 'You may eat from every tree in the garden,

17 but not from the tree of the knowledge of good and evil; for on the day that you eat it, you will certainly die.'

✵ Man is now placed by the LORD God in a garden *in Eden* (verse 8). There is little doubt that here, and in verses 10–14, Eden is intended to be a place *away to the east*. This vague reference is further defined by the mention of a river *flowing from* or rising in Eden, a river which *branched into four streams* (verse 10). Of these four streams, two, *Pishon* and *Gihon*, appear only here in the Old Testament as names of rivers. The identity of these rivers, as well as that of the countries associated with them, *Havilah* and *Cush*, has been endlessly and inconclusively discussed. Nor is there certainty as to the precise meaning of the precious substances found in the land of *Havilah*. Both words should probably be translated, following the Septuagint, as precious stones, *bdellium* and *cornelians*, although the Hebrew word translated *bdellium* can also refer to a type of gum resin (so N.E.B. footnote). The two rivers which can be positively identified, *Tigris* and

[a] *Or* frankincense.   [b] *Or* gum resin.

Euphrates, both rise in the mountains to the north of the Mesopotamian valley. It seems unwise to look further afield for the mysterious *Pishon* and *Gihon*. One difficulty in this is that elsewhere in the Old Testament Havilah and Cush appear as place names associated with the region of Upper Egypt and Ethiopia (cp. Gen. 10: 7; Ezek. 29: 10); this has led to *Pishon* and *Gihon* being identified with the two branches of the Nile. Much must be pure speculation, especially when we do not know whether the writer had in his mind anything remotely resembling the now known geography of the Middle East. Two further considerations are relevant.

(i) Only in verses 8 and 10–14 (and verses 10–14 may be a learned antiquarian addition to the story) is Eden definitely a geographical term. Elsewhere in the Old Testament, notably in Ezek. 28, there are references which range far beyond what is recounted here and which point to Eden being a mythological and religious idea rather than a place on the map. In Ezek. 28, Eden, the garden of God, is located on the holy mountain of God (Ezek. 28: 14, 16), and in this garden there is a king. We seem to have echoes here of a theme found in Mesopotamian mythology of the king as primordial man placed in a divine garden as the guardian of the tree of life. Some have interpreted 'man' in Gen. 2–3 and in Ps. 8 in such royal terms. This seems to outrun the evidence. It is not only the garden which has traditional religious associations. We know that *El*, the supreme god of the Canaanite pantheon, had his dwelling place at the source of two rivers.

(ii) In itself the phrase translated *the garden of Eden* (2: 15; 3: 23, 24) need mean no more than 'the garden of delight', that garden of paradise where once all was harmony. The mythological traits and the religious significance of the garden are far more important than its possible geographical location.

9. In the garden, in addition to ordinary trees, *pleasant to look at and good for food*, there are two mysterious trees *the tree of life and the tree of the knowledge of good and evil*. Round

these two trees the story weaves its drama and explores something of the mystery which is man.

15–17. These are key verses for our understanding of the whole narrative but they raise difficult problems of interpretation. It is noticeable that *the tree of life* mentioned in verse 9 has disappeared from the scene, to reappear at 3: 5 only after tragedy has struck. Unlike the emphasis in certain Mesopotamian myths the problem of man in Gen. 2–3 is not diagnosed as his striving after elusive immortality. Man is placed in the garden not only *to till it and care for it* (verse 15), but to learn the lesson of living responsibly under an authority greater than himself. He is forbidden to touch the fruit of *the tree of the knowledge of good and evil* (verse 17, cp. 3: 5; otherwise described as 'the tree in the middle of the garden' 3: 3).

What is this tree? 'Knowledge' and 'knowing' in the Old Testament may refer to the broad range of human experience, personal experience at its deepest level including sexual experience, as well as moral and intellectual experience. Thus in Gen. 4: 1 'The man lay with Eve his wife' may be more literally translated 'the man *knew* Eve his wife'. Similarly *good and evil* are not necessarily moral terms; they may have emotional and aesthetic meanings, cp. 2: 9 where the trees are said to be 'good for food' just as in English we talk of something tasting good.

Gen. 2–3 has frequently been given a sexual interpretation. Several features in the narrative may be interpreted as pointing in this direction. There is the sense of shame at their own nakedness which comes to the man and the woman after they have tasted the forbidden fruit (3: 10–11). The penalty inflicted upon Eve for her disobedience is related to her sexuality, pain associated with childbirth (3: 16). There is further a tempting parallel with the Gilgamesh epic. Gilgamesh's companion Enkidu is depicted at the outset as a child of nature, friend of all the creatures of the wild. Yielding to the wiles of a courtesan, he loses his oneness with the natural world, but, so it is claimed, he has acquired wisdom. The courtesan says to him 'You are wise, Enkidu, you are like a god', cp. the words of temptation in 3: 5 'as soon as you eat it, your eyes will be opened and you will be like gods knowing both good and evil'. The most acceptable form of this sexual interpretation reads the narrative not as a polemic against sex, but as a warning against the misuse, the deification of sex in the worship orgies of Canaanite fertility cults. The seductiveness of this type of religion, with its sacred prostitutes, was a recurring temptation to the Hebrews from the time when they began to settle in the land of Canaan.

knowledge of good and evil has also been taken to mean knowledge of the powerful spells and incantations by which man seeks to control the friendly and hostile forces in the world around him. Such dabbling in the occult, common enough in Babylonian religion, is rigorously forbidden in other Old Testament passages (cp. Deut. 18: 14).

The view taken here is that neither of these interpretations does justice to the narrative taken as a whole. The phrase *good and evil* is best taken as a Hebrew idiom whereby opposites are used to convey the idea of 'everything' (cp. Gen. 24: 50 where the literal rendering 'we cannot speak to you evil or good' means 'we have nothing to say'). *the knowledge of good and evil*, forbidden to man, therefore, is the totality of knowledge. Man is being warned that he is subject to certain limitations. He is not omniscient; he is not all-powerful in himself. He can choose to accept his lot as a creature under the authority of God or he can attempt to be 'Mr Know All' and go it alone. He can acknowledge his dependence upon God or he can assert his independence from God – and accept the consequences. The consequences are momentous: *for in the day that you eat from it you will certainly die* (verse 17), or perhaps better 'you are doomed to die'. The way of self is the way of death:

> 'Lord of himself – that heritage of woe'
> (Byron, *Lara* c. 1. ii). ✻

THE LONELINESS AND NEED OF MAN

18 Then the LORD God said, 'It is not good for the man to be
19 alone. I will provide a partner for him.' So God formed
out of the ground all the wild animals and all the birds
of heaven. He brought them to the man to see what
he would call them, and whatever the man called each
20 living creature, that was its name. Thus the man gave
names to all cattle, to the birds of heaven, and to every
wild animal; but for the man himself no partner had yet
21 been found. And so the LORD God put the man into a
trance, and while he slept, he took one of his ribs and
22 closed the flesh over the place. The LORD God then built
up the rib, which he had taken out of the man, into a
23 woman. He brought her to the man, and the man said:

> 'Now this, at last—
> bone from my bones,
> flesh from my flesh!—
> this shall be called woman,[a]
> for from man[b] was this taken.'

24 That is why a man leaves his father and mother and is
25 united to his wife, and the two become one flesh. Now
they were both naked, the man and his wife, but they
had no feeling of shame towards one another.

* This section opens with the recognition that man in himself is incomplete. He needs a *partner* or suitable helper. Then
follows the account of how God forms out of the ground *all
the wild animals and all the birds of heaven* (verse 19). Each is
brought in turn to man to be given its name, *whatever the*

[a] *Heb.* ishshah.   [b] *Heb.* ish.

man called each living creature, that was its name (verse 19).
This giving of a name is an Old Testament way of declaring
man's power over the rest of creation; it is the J parallel to
the theme of man's dominion which is heard in the creation
hymn in Gen. 1: 26–7. Some scholars believe that the narrative is here recounting a series of unsuccessful experiments to
find a partner for man. This is doubtful. The existence of
these other creatures serves to underline man's sense of
loneliness. He has power over them, but none fill his need;
for the man himself no partner had yet been found (verse 20).

21–3. This partner is to be found not in anything brought
to man; it comes from himself, part of himself, a new wonder
created by God while the man is in *a trance* or deep sleep, a
word used elsewhere in the Old Testament to describe a
condition in which man receives a vision or message which
comes from God unasked (cp. Gen. 15: 12; Job 4: 13). The
delightfully naïve picture of the LORD God taking a rib from
the unconscious man and building it up into a woman should
not blind us to the deep truth being conveyed. This truth
is underlined in a brief, rhythmic poem in verse 23. *this, at
last* – notice how the word *this* echoes three times across the
poem – *this* is the partner, *'ishshāh woman*, so called because
she has been taken from *'īsh man* or male. This is not a piece
of scientific etymology; the words *'ishshāh* and *'īsh* come
from two different roots in Hebrew, just as female and
male do in English. It is one example among many in the
Old Testament of a popular play on words, based on similarity of sound (cp. Gen. 17: 5). With greater etymo-
logical justification we talk in English of man and woman,
that is, wife of man. Yet this popular play on words
springs out of a unique relationship:

> *bone from my bones,*
> *flesh from my flesh!* —

a relationship whose meaning the narrator now explains.
24. *That is why*: this is the first of a series of personal com-

ments by the narrator of the Genesis traditions; others will be found at 10: 9; 21: 31; 32: 32. In them, he finds in some incident the explanation for a religious or social practice with which he is familiar. Here it is the marriage relationship, in which a man and a woman realize that oneness which belongs to their God-given nature. They *become one flesh*, one personality. *flesh* means more than the physical side of life; it is the medium through which the whole personality communicates its varied emotions, longings, joys and fears; cp. Ps. 84: 2

'my whole being (lit. my heart and my flesh) cries out
    with joy
to the living God'.

No doubt a Hebrew lawyer would have framed verse 24 differently, to point out that in fact it is the woman who leaves her home to be united to the man. Some have seen in this verse echoes of a matriarchal type of society. But the narrator is neither lawyer nor sociologist. He is grappling on a religious level with the need and loneliness of man, therefore it is natural enough for him to talk of the man being *united to his wife*.

25. Man and woman live in a world of total innocence. Their nakedness brings to them *no feeling of shame*. Such feelings of shame are the by-product of the consciousness of evil which has not yet entered the world. ✳

DISOBEDIENCE

3 The serpent was more crafty than any wild creature that the LORD God had made. He said to the woman, 'Is it true that God has forbidden you to eat from any tree in
2 the garden?' The woman answered the serpent, 'We
3 may eat the fruit of any tree in the garden, except for the tree in the middle of the garden; God has forbidden us either to eat or to touch the fruit of that; if we do, we

shall die.' The serpent said, 'Of course you will not die. 4
God knows that as soon as you eat it, your eyes will be 5
opened and you will be like gods[a] knowing both good
and evil.' When the woman saw that the fruit of the tree 6
was good to eat, and that it was pleasing to the eye and
tempting to contemplate, she took some and ate it. She
also gave her husband some and he ate it. Then the eyes 7
of both of them were opened and they discovered that
they were naked; so they stitched fig-leaves together and
made themselves loincloths.

* *The serpent* plays a prominent role in the religious mythology of the ancient world. We know of serpent gods, of
serpents closely associated with the tree of life and a variety of
fertility rituals. In the epic of Gilgamesh a serpent robs
Gilgamesh of the plant whose name is 'man becomes young
in old age'. Several poetic passages in the Old Testament
preserve echoes of an ancient cosmological story in which
God does battle against primordial forces of chaos symbolized
by a sea-serpent (cp. Isa. 27: 1). But just as the creation hymn
in Gen. 1 is remarkably restrained in its use of creation
mythology, so here the serpent seems to have been demoted.
He is merely one of the wild creatures that the LORD God had
made, different only in that he is *more crafty* (verse 1). Certainly there is no suggestion in the narrative that he is a
supernatural, demonic figure to be equated with Satan.
This development comes much later in Jewish and Christian
thinking. The serpent indeed is almost incidental to the central
thrust of the story. In the dialogue between the serpent and
the woman we are overhearing a struggle which is going on
in the mind of the woman, a struggle between innocence and
temptation.

1–3. Temptation begins with an apparently innocuous

[a] Or God.

question. *Is it true that God has forbidden . . .?* a request for information, but one which insinuates that God has been unnecessarily authoritarian. The woman immediately springs to God's defence. Only the fruit of one tree, *the tree in the middle of the garden* (verse 3) is forbidden, under penalty of death.

or to touch the fruit of that: this addition to the prohibition as originally stated in 2: 17 has led certain scholars to suggest that the woman herself is now beginning to overplay God's strictness. It may, however, be no more than a stylistic variation on the prohibition against eating.

4f. Having drawn the woman into conversation the serpent now scoffingly attacks not the prohibition, but what he claims lies behind it. It is rooted, he suggests, in God's envy – a widespread idea in the ancient world. God wants to keep something from you; and it is yours for the taking. Eat, and far from dying, *your eyes will be opened and you will be like gods* or better, with N.E.B. footnote 'God' – it is difficult to see why Heb. *'elōhīm* should be translated as a plural this once in the entire narrative. If we retain the translation *gods*, then *knowing good and evil* may well be a description of these supernatural beings; they, unlike mere mortals, know good and evil. If we read 'God', *knowing good and evil* is best taken with *you; you*, man and woman, you will be like God, you will know good and evil. Either way, the temptation is an appeal to that human arrogance which will accept no limitations, which insists on knowing everything.

6f. With great economy of words and without moralizing, verses 6–7 describe tragedy. The fruit of the tree is *good to eat*, it is attractive to the eye, and the more the woman looks at it the more attractive it becomes. It is *tempting to contemplate*, a translation which makes good sense in context, may claim support from the Septuagint but which means giving to a Hebrew word a meaning which it does not have elsewhere in the Old Testament, although it is found in later

Hebrew and in Aramaic. More commonly, and in line with
the usual meaning of the word in the Old Testament, the
fruit of the tree is described as 'a means to wisdom'.

she took some and ate: the man followed her example, and
immediately the garden of delight becomes the garden of
disenchantment. Their eyes are indeed opened, as the serpent
had claimed, but what they see brings only a sense of shame,
they discovered that they were naked. Innocence has fled. They
cover their nakedness with *fig-leaves* (contrast 2: 25). What
they cannot cover is the nakedness of their guilt before God. *

INTERROGATION

The man and his wife heard the sound of the LORD   8
God walking in the garden at the time of the evening
breeze and hid from the LORD God among the trees of the
garden. But the LORD God called to the man and said to   9
him, 'Where are you?' He replied, 'I heard the sound   10
as you were walking in the garden, and I was afraid
because I was naked, and I hid myself.' God answered,   11
'Who told you that you were naked? Have you eaten
from the tree which I forbade you?' The man said, 'The   12
woman you gave me for a companion, she gave me fruit
from the tree and I ate it.'

* The tragedy is underlined. God had hitherto been the
gracious focus and source of man's life: God had made him
(2: 7f), God had set him in the garden (2: 15ff), God had
given him authority over the animals (2: 19f), God had
provided him with a partner (2: 21ff). Now the mere *sound
of the LORD God walking in the garden* (verse 8) makes the
man and his wife scurry into futile hiding.

8. *sound* is preferable to 'voice' (A.V.). The reference is
not to anything God says. He does not need to speak to

bring home to man and woman a sense of guilt. The *sound of him moving in the garden is enough.*

at the time of the evening breeze: lit. 'towards (or at) the wind of the day'. Septuagint correctly interprets as 'in the evening' towards sundown when the heat of the day is cooled by the evening breeze.

9–12. God's interrogation begins with the man. The rhetorical question '*Where are you?*' evokes an evasive answer. The evasion is met by two directly accusatory questions: '*Who told you that you were naked? Have you eaten . . .?*' (verse 11). The man admits '*I ate it*' (verse 12), but tries to wash his hands of responsibility for what has happened by blaming the woman and God, '*The woman you gave me . . . she gave me fruit*' (verse 12).

Interrogation turns to the woman, and she blames the serpent. 'Passing the buck' is a game as old as human nature. ✶

JUDGEMENT

13 Then the LORD God said to the woman, 'What is this that you have done?' The woman said, 'The serpent
14 tricked me, and I ate.' Then the LORD God said to the serpent:

'Because you have done this you are accursed
   more than all cattle and all wild creatures.
On your belly you shall crawl, and dust you shall eat
   all the days of your life.
15 I will put enmity between you and the woman,
   between your brood and hers.
They shall strike at your head,
   and you shall strike at their heel.'

16 To the woman he said:

'I will increase your labour and your groaning,

and in labour you shall bear children.
You shall be eager[a] for your husband,
and he shall be your master.'

And to the man he said: 17
'Because you have listened to your wife
and have eaten from the tree which I forbade you,
accursed shall be the ground on your account.
With labour you shall win your food from it
all the days of your life.
It will grow thorns and thistles for you,   18
none but wild plants for you to eat.
You shall gain your bread by the sweat of your brow   19
until you return to the ground;
for from it you were taken.
Dust you are, to dust you shall return.'

✼ Interrogation passes swiftly into judgement, beginning
with the serpent and proceeding through woman to man,
thus coming round full circle to where the interrogation
began. The solemnity of the judgement is stressed by the
rhythmic speech in which it is delivered. There is a strong
aetiological element (see p. 10) in the judgement. It provides
answers to a whole series of puzzling 'whys'. Why is the
serpent such an odd creature crawling around in the dust?
(verse 14). Why is there an instinctive mutual antipathy
between the snake and man? (verse 15). Why is childbearing
painful? Why is man the dominant partner in the marriage
relationship? (verse 16). Why is the life of the peasant farmer
so hard? (verse 17). Such 'whys' spring out of the common
experience of life in the ancient world. They may not be our
'whys'. We would have a different, more scientific approach
to some of the questions. It is important to note, however,

[a] *Or* feel an urge.

that the narrator's primary interest is not aetiological. He is a theologian wrestling with the many faceted problem of evil in a God-created world. He takes human responsibility with deadly seriousness. He finds in man's attempt to overstep the bounds of his creaturely dependence upon God, in man's grasping at autonomy, the root of all evil and friction in the world.

14–15. Judgement on the serpent. The opening words look back to the beginning of chapter 3. Just as the serpent was 'more crafty' (3: 1) than any wild creature, so now he is *accursed more than all cattle and all wild creatures* (verse 14). Although the serpent is merely one of the wild creatures in the story, the role he plays makes him inevitably symbolic of evil, and verse 15 has often been regarded as the first pointer in the Old Testament to the ultimate triumph of good over evil. In the *enmity* and subsequent conflict *between you and the woman, between your brood and hers* (lit. your seed and her seed) certain early Jewish interpreters saw a reference to the victory of the Jewish community over evil in the days of the Messiah. Christian interpreters saw in *the woman* a reference to the Virgin Mary, and in 'her seed' a reference to Christ, an interpretation which was strengthened by the Vulgate reading 'she' instead of *They* in the second half of verse 15. This outruns the evidence. The verse speaks not of victory, but of continuing conflict, with characteristic blows being inflicted. People *strike at* or bruise the serpent's head, the serpent *strikes at* their heel. The harmony and peace of the garden has been irrevocably shattered; perpetual conflict, a deadly struggle with evil now begins.

16. Judgement on the woman. Just as the woman, instead of being the intended true partner, had enticed the man into evil, so she is punished in her womanhood, in her relationship to the man. The punishment is twofold:

(*a*) *your labour and your groaning:* or better 'your labour and your conception', your travail in childbirth. The pangs of childbirth are to be intense. They become in the Old Testament synonymous for extreme anguish; see, for example, Jer. 6: 24 where the threat of destruction at the hands of a cruel and pitiless enemy evokes from the community the following response:

'agony grips us, the anguish of a woman in labour'.

(b) *You shall be eager for your husband:* lit. your desire (or 'longing', see Song of Songs 7: 10 where the sexual overtones in this word are evident) will be for your husband. This ardent desire, however, is to bring the woman not into partnership but into subjection. The deepest human relationship has thus been perverted.

17–19. Judgement on the man. Judgement strikes at the nerve of man's existence – work. The ground he tills is *accursed.* He has his own *labour* or travail – the word used is the same as that used to describe the woman's travail in verse 16. Instead of a garden of plenty to till and to care (3: 15), by the sweat of his brow he has to struggle for existence with a land which produces *thorns and thistles* and *wild plants.* Some scholars find in these verses a double tradition, the one (verse 17 and most of verse 19) reflecting the hard life of the peasant farmer, the other (verse 18 and the concluding sentence of verse 19) reflecting the life of the nomad of the desert steppe. This is possible, but far from certain. It is more important to notice the close link between man and his physical environment. Because of what man did the ground has become *accursed.* For good and for ill in Old Testament thinking, man and his environment interact on one another. Deut. 28 contains a series of blessings and curses which stress this interaction. A community obedient to God receives blessing in city and in countryside:

'A blessing on the fruit of your body, the fruit of your land and of your cattle, the offspring of your herds and of your lambing flocks. A blessing on your basket and your kneading-trough' (Deut. 28: 4–5).

A disobedient community experiences a similar curse, see Deut. 28: 16–18. In Rom. 8: 22 Paul says that 'the whole created universe groans in all its parts as if in the pangs of childbirth', waiting for the dawning of a New Age when both man and the world in which he lives will be renewed. Theology and ecology are running partners.

Judgement shatters man's pretensions. He had aimed to 'become like gods' (3: 5); in the outcome he is destined to return to the ground from which he came, see comment on 2: 7;

Dust you are, and to dust you shall return (verse 19).

He grasps at omniscience, he finds death.   ✻

EXPULSION

20 The man called his wife Eve[a] because she was the
21 mother of all who live. The LORD God made tunics of
22 skins for Adam and his wife and clothed them. He said,
'The man has become like one of us, knowing good and evil; what if he now reaches out his hand and takes fruit from the tree of life also, eats it and lives for ever?'
23 So the LORD God drove him out of the garden of Eden
24 to till the ground from which he had been taken. He cast him out, and to the east of the garden of Eden he stationed the cherubim and a sword whirling and flashing to guard the way to the tree of life.

✻ The judgement on the serpent, the woman and the man each contain a threat of future punishment. But judgement also has its present reality, the expulsion from the garden of delight. This expulsion, and the reason for it, are described in verses 22–4. But what of verses 20–1? In some respects they

[a] *That is* Life.

are puzzling. Is verse 21, for example, merely a variant tradition of verse 7? The view taken here is that verses 20-1 are best seen as a prelude to the story of the expulsion from the garden, a prelude which gives us further insight into the mind of the narrator.

20. The man now asserts his authority over his wife by naming her *Eve*, Heb. *ḥawwāh*. The explanation of this name as *the mother of all who live—ḥāy* being the Hebrew word for life – is the comment of the narrator and gives us the clue as to his intentions. Many scholars, from the time of the early Jewish commentators onwards, have claimed that *ḥawwāh* should be linked linguistically with the Aramaic word for snake *ḥīwyā*, and that for obvious reasons the woman was called 'snake mother'. If this is so, then the narrator has deliberately altered the tradition so that the name *ḥawwāh* becomes a symbol of hope. Even in the midst of the divinely inflicted penalty of death, there is continuing life: here is *the mother of all who live*.

21. Again it would be wrong to regard this verse as merely aetiological, providing an explanation for the wearing of clothes. It is God who makes for man and his wife *tunics of skins*. Independent they may have tried to be, but God's hand is still stretched out to meet their immediate need. It is hard to see why the N.E.B. introduces *Adam* as a personal name in this verse. The Hebrew text certainly reads 'man' and not 'the man', but the same holds true in 2: 20, and 3: 17 where N.E.B. has translated 'the man'.

22. For the first time since its brief mention in 2: 9 (see p. 33) *the tree of life* reappears in the story. The theme of man's search for elusive immortality re-enters the story only when the problem and the tragedy of man have been analysed in other terms. Having grasped at independence, having become like one of us, possessing all knowledge, man will naturally know the location of the mysterious *tree of life* and will be tempted to reach out and take its fruit. So man must be expelled from Eden.

23. *So the LORD God drove him out:* the verb here translated *drove him out* comes from the same root as the word translated *reaches* in verse 22. Lest man 'reaches' out his hand to grasp the fruit of the tree of life, Eden has to be put 'out of reach'.

24. The way to the tree of life is barred by a divine security guard. *the cherubim:* in Akkadian sources *karibu* (cherubim) appear as mythological figures, minor deities, half human, half animal. Royal thrones were sometimes flanked on either side by winged lions with human heads. In the Old Testament cherubim appear as winged attendants of Yahweh:

'He rode on a cherub, he flew through the air;
he swooped on the wings of the wind' (Ps. 18: 10),

and as guardians of sacred shrines and objects such as the ark (Exod. 25: 18; 1 Kings 8: 6). In addition to the *cherubim* there is *a sword whirling and flashing*, a phrase which likewise may have a mythological background; many of the gods in ancient near eastern pantheons having their own weapons of war.

The whole narrative from 2: 15 – 3: 24 is one of tragedy; of a dream that was shattered by the self-will of man who makes a bid for independence and loses his own true life. This, for the narrator, is not ancient story but an ever present reality. Religious motifs, from many different circles in the Ancient Near East, are taken by the narrator and transformed in the crucible of his own experience. Faith, like poetry, communicates some of its deepest truths through symbols which, steeped in tradition, are yet capable of being given ever new meaning. ✶

CAIN AND ABEL

4 The man lay with his wife Eve, and she conceived and gave birth to Cain. She said, 'With the help of the LORD
2 I have brought a man into being.' Afterwards she had another child, his brother Abel. Abel was a shepherd

and Cain a tiller of the soil. The day came when Cain 3
brought some of the produce of the soil as a gift to the
LORD; and Abel brought some of the first-born of his 4
flock, the fat portions of them.*a* The LORD received Abel
and his gift with favour; but Cain and his gift he did not 5
receive. Cain was very angry and his face fell. Then 6
the LORD said to Cain, 'Why are you so angry and cast
down?

If you do well, you are accepted,*b*   7
if not, sin is a demon crouching at the door.
It shall be eager for you, and you will be mastered
by it.'*c*

Cain said to his brother Abel, 'Let us go into the open 8
country.'*d* While they were there, Cain attacked his
brother Abel and murdered him. Then the LORD said to 9
Cain, 'Where is your brother Abel?' Cain answered, 'I
do not know. Am I my brother's keeper?' The LORD said, 10
'What have you done? Hark! your brother's blood that
has been shed is crying out to me from the ground. Now 11
you are accursed, and banished from*e* the ground which
has opened its mouth wide to receive your brother's
blood, which you have shed. When you till the ground, 12
it will no longer yield you its wealth. You shall be a
vagrant and a wanderer on earth.' Cain said to the LORD, 13
'My punishment is heavier than I can bear; thou hast 14
driven me today from the ground, and I must hide myself
from thy presence. I shall be a vagrant and a wanderer

[a] *Or* some of the first-born, that is the sucklings, of his flock.
[b] *Or* you hold your head up.   [c] *Or* but you must master it.
[d] Let us . . . country: *so Sam.; Heb. om.*
[e] and banished from: *or* more than (*cp. 3: 17*).

49

15 on earth, and anyone who meets me can kill me.' The LORD answered him, 'No: if anyone kills Cain, Cain shall be avenged sevenfold.' So the LORD put a mark on Cain, in order that anyone meeting him should not
16 kill him. Then Cain went out from the LORD's presence and settled in the land of Nod*ᵃ ᵇ* to the east of Eden.

* If taken on its own, the story of Cain and Abel may be interpreted in many different ways. Cain may be regarded as the ancestor of the Kenites, a tribal group whose relationship to the Hebrews was somewhat ambivalent in Old Testament times. They seem to have lived on the fringes of the settled land and to have been regarded by some as a gipsy-like group of wandering smiths (Judg. 1: 16; 4: 11, 17); *qayīn* in Hebrew can mean smith. To some the story tells of the clash between two different vocations, that of the peasant farmer (Cain) and that of the herdsman (Abel); to others it asserts the superiority of animal sacrifice over any other type of sacrifice (see verses 4–5). Should it be regarded as an aetiological story explaining the custom of blood revenge and the tribal identification marks which made it possible (see verse 15)? Or may it be regarded as the Old Testament parallel to the Roman story of Romulus and Remus, a story explaining why human sacrifice is considered necessary at the foundation of a city or state? Certain strange features in the story, such as the *demon* in verse 7, have been traced back to ritual practices which we find in Babylonian religion.

It has to be admitted that any attempt to take the story out of its present context and trace its prehistory is doomed to be purely speculative. The J narrator has once again taken what may be a very ancient story and adapted it for his own purpose. That purpose is theological. The breakdown in the relationship of harmony between man and God leads inevit-

[a] *That is* Wandering.
[b] and settled . . . Nod: *or* and he lived as a wanderer in the land.

ably to tragedy in human relationships. The 'self' which has asserted itself against God, now asserts itself against a brother.

1. The narrator here provides the link with the story of the garden. *The man lay with his wife:* Heb. 'knew' his wife, see comment on 2: 15–17. Eve now begins to fulfil the promise implicit in 3: 20 that she will be the mother of all who live. She produces a son, *Cain*, his name, *qayīn* in Hebrew, being a play on the similarity in sound to the Hebrew word translated '*I have brought . . . into being*', *qānītī*.

brought . . . into being: an improvement on the traditional 'gotten' (R.S.V.) since a cognate word in the Canaanite texts from Ugarit in north Syria means create, give birth to (see Gen. 14: 19, 22).

The sentence beginning *With the help of the LORD* is of very doubtful meaning. Nowhere else in the Old Testament is 'man' used as a description of a male child. The translation *With the help of* assumes giving an unusual meaning to a Hebrew preposition. Most of the versions imply some such meaning, but the Aramaic Targum by a slight change of the text renders 'from the LORD', indicating the divine source of this new life.

2–4. The name *Abel*, Heb. *hebel*, is left unexplained. It has been connected with a cognate Akkadian word meaning son. In the Old Testament, *hebel* indicates something that is fleeting or insubstantial, such as breath. It is the word which occurs in the motto text of Ecclesiastes, which N.E.B. renders 'Emptiness, emptiness' (Eccles. 1: 2). Here it may be intended to indicate the swift fate that befalls *Abel*.

The brothers pursue their respective callings, Abel *a shepherd*, Cain *a tiller of the soil*. Each in turn brings to God a sacrifice appropriate to his way of life, Cain *some of the produce of the soil*, Abel *some of the first-born of his flock*.

the fat portions of them: the choicest parts of the animal, regularly offered to God on the altar, see Lev. 3: 3ff. N.E.B. footnote derives this word from the Hebrew word for 'milk', hence 'sucklings'; see 1 Sam. 7: 9 where Samuel offers as a sacrifice a 'sucking lamb'.

5–6. The narrative here is very terse and restrained. It does not tell us how the LORD indicated his acceptance of Abel's offering, nor why Cain's was rejected.

5. *his face fell:* a literal translation of the phrase which in verse 6 is rendered *cast down*. A verb expressing vexation or disappointment would be appropriate in both cases.

7. In three lines of rhythmic prose the LORD challenges Cain.

If you do well . . . if not: this implies that what was wrong with Cain was not the type of sacrifice he brought, but the spirit in which he brought it.

you are accepted: Heb. literally 'lifting up'. Assuming that we understand the word 'face' after 'lifting up', then this can mean either (i) the opposite of 'his face fell' (verse 5), hence the N.E.B. footnote 'you hold your head up', you will have reason to be glad; or (ii) to lift up the face, in the sense of being gracious to another person, hence the N.E.B. *you are accepted* or you will be accepted. This latter rendering makes perhaps best sense in context.

sin is a demon: the translation *demon* assumes that Heb. *rōbēts* is a noun corresponding to the Akkadian *rabisu*, demon. Sin thus lurks, demon-like, at the door, ready to spring.

It shall be eager for you: see comment on 3: 16.

and you will be mastered by it: this translation, by changing the vowels of the Hebrew text, assumes that the final sentence is a statement of fact. Evil is attacking Cain and has him at its mercy. N.E.B. footnote retains the traditional reading, 'but you must master it', a challenge to Cain to fight against the evil which threatens him.

8. The Hebrew text hardly makes sense. Most of the versions, including the Samaritan and Septuagint, have a longer text which tells us what *Cain said to his brother Abel.*

9–10. Crime, in this case a brother's murder, is immediately followed, as in 3: 9ff, by interrogation. Attitudes have hardened. Instead of attempting to excuse his conduct, Cain denies all knowledge of what has happened in words which have become a classic expression for irresponsibility, '*Am I my brother's keeper?*' But guilt cannot be concealed from the LORD. The shed blood cries out *from the ground*, demanding justice and vengeance. Both here and in the vivid language of verse 11, *the ground which has opened its mouth wide to receive your brother's blood*, there may be echoes of a primitive religious belief in which the ground, equated with the entrance to the underworld or the abode of the dead – Sheol in the Old Testament – opens its mouth to swallow the blood of its victims. But death, a powerful god in many a pantheon, has been dethroned. Nowhere lies outside the knowledge and power of the LORD (cp. Isa. 26: 21).

11. For the third time in these opening chapters of Genesis (see 3: 14 and 3: 17) judgement is pronounced in the form of a curse. Implicit in the curse there is often the idea of someone being banned from something. Thus a phrase which in Hebrew may be literally translated 'you are cursed from the ground' is rendered by the N.E.B. *you are accursed, and banished from the ground*. N.E.B. footnote implies that the curse placed on Cain is greater than the curse pronounced on the ground in 3: 17; in context a less likely rendering.

12. Cain's punishment is twofold:

(*a*) his vocation as a farmer is destroyed, the earth *will no longer yield you its wealth*;

(*b*) he is condemned to be *a vagrant and a wanderer*, a homeless outlaw.

13. '*My punishment is heavier that I can bear*': a plea for mercy. The sentence may also be rendered with some of the versions including Septuagint 'My iniquity (or guilt) is too great to be forgiven', in which case Cain is recognizing the enormity of his crime.

14. Cain's fear: on the run from man and from God, he will be a ready victim for anyone who cares to strike him down.

15. A remarkable theological climax to the story. Cain is cursed and outlawed, but not separated from the LORD's

protection. Cain may have tried to wash his hands of Abel, but the LORD does not wash his hands of Cain. He remains Cain's keeper. He protects him with a solemn threat of vengeance, and places on him a *mark* or sign to indicate that he is a protected person.

No: or 'in that case'. This is the way in which the versions interpret a Hebrew word which is traditionally translated 'therefore'.

16. *from the LORD's presence:* this must not be taken to mean that the LORD is thought of as being present only in the vicinity of the garden. Cain's interview with the LORD has ended; he withdraws, as one might after an audience with royalty.

Cain goes forth to banishment, to dwell *in the land of Nod.* Nod, which in Hebrew means 'wandering' (see N.E.B. footnote), is nowhere else found in the Old Testament as a place name. It is used here to convey the idea that Cain has become a 'homeless wanderer', out in the far distant, unknown region, *east of Eden.* ✶

THE FAMILY TREE OF CAIN

17 Then Cain lay with his wife; and she conceived and bore Enoch. Cain was then building a city, which he
18 named Enoch after his son. Enoch begot Irad; Irad begot Mehujael; Mehujael begot Methushael; Methushael begot Lamech.

19 Lamech married two wives, one named Adah and the
20 other Zillah. Adah bore Jabal who was the ancestor of
21 herdsmen who live in tents; and his brother's name was Jubal; he was the ancestor of those who play the harp and
22 pipe. Zillah, the other wife, bore Tubal-cain, the master of all coppersmiths and blacksmiths, and Tubal-cain's
23 sister was Naamah. Lamech said to his wives:

'Adah and Zillah, listen to me;
wives of Lamech, mark what I say:
I kill a man for wounding me,
a young man for a blow.
Cain may be avenged seven times,   24
but Lamech seventy-seven.'

* This is the first of a series of 'family trees' which Old Testament writers use to describe not only the passing of the generations, but also certain characteristic features of life which they believe to have emerged in different historical epochs. This family tree of Cain seems to be a very ancient piece of tradition. Many of the names in it reappear, not in the same order, and sometimes in slightly different forms, in chapter 5. Common to both lists are the names Enoch (4: 17f; 5: 18ff), Lamech (4: 18ff; 5: 25ff) and in slightly variant form, Irad (4: 18) and Jared (5: 18), Mehujael (4: 18f) and Mahalalel (5: 15), Methushael (4: 18) and Methuselah (5: 21). Both lists may derive from a common source. It would hardly be surprising if during centuries of oral transmission variations appeared, particularly in names of uncertain meaning and origin. Detailed discussion of the names will be found in the larger commentaries noted on p. 113. Sumerian tradition preserved two lists of kings who reigned before the flood, one of them containing eight names, as does this family tree of Cain, the other ten names, as does the family tree in chapter 5.

There are difficulties in reading this section as the direct continuation of the Cain and Abel story. On such an assumption the heckler's favourite question 'Where did Cain get his wife from?' has no obvious answer unless we follow early Jewish tradition, found in the book of Jubilees 4: 1, and say that he married his sister. Further, unless the flood tradition in Gen. 6–8 is of purely local significance, not indicating a total cultural break, there seems little point in tracing the origin of various cultural and sociological factors back beyond the flood to the sons of Lamech (verses 19-22). We can only understand this family tree if we remember that J is using old traditions for his own religious purposes.

17. *Cain lay with his wife:* see comment on 2: 15-17; 4: 25. The description of Cain as *building a city* is not easily reconcilable with the 'vagrant and wanderer' of 4: 12. A strongly cultural interest, however, is evident in this family tree. To Cain is traced the origin of settled community existence.

Enoch: see commentary on 5: 21f. Outside these family trees Enoch appears as a personal name associated with the Midianites in Gen. 25: 4 and with the family of Reuben in Gen. 46: 9.

19. *Lamech married two wives:* the fact of polygamy is noted without comment or moral judgement. It was accepted social custom in patriarchal times (see Gen. 29) and in later Israel (2 Sam. 3: 2-5).

20-2. In many religious traditions prominent features of social life and culture are traced back to gods or semi-divine heroes. Canaanite tradition, for example, as reflected in the Ugaritic texts, makes a god Kathar-Hasis, 'Skilful and Percipient One', the patron saint of metal workers. It is in keeping with the strongly monotheistic ethos of the Old Testament that it traces such factors to a purely human origin, to the sons of *Lamech*.

20. *Jabal . . . the ancestor of herdsmen who live in tents:* lit. 'the father of those who dwell in tents and cattle' (A.V.), the pastoral nomad whose wealth is his herd.

21. *Jubal . . . the ancestor of those who play the harp and the pipe:* the inventor of music, both stringed and wind instruments.

22. *Tubal-cain:* Tubal the smith (see p. 50).

the master of all coppersmiths and blacksmiths: a difficult phrase in Hebrew. With a slight change in text it may be rendered 'the forger of copper and iron tools' (R.S.V.).

23-4. Civilization advances, but what of man? It can

hardly be accidental that J has placed as the climax to this family the so-called Song of Lamech, a brief poem which breathes the spirit of a proud, implacable vengeance. The Song is a very good example of Hebrew poetic style, its three double lines making effective use of thought parallelism: for example in the first double line, *Adah and Zillah* echoed by *wives of Lamech*, and *listen to me* echoed by *mark what I say*. Cain may have killed a brother in cold blood, he may have been protected by the threat of sevenfold vengeance; but Lamech acts with almost unrestrained ferocity, prepared to exact *seventy-seven* fold vengeance for any slight. Was Jesus recalling this passage when he told his disciples that they must be prepared to forgive seventy times seven (Matt. 18: 22)? Civilization advances, but man is caught up in an ever accelerating 'Rake's Progress'. On this note the family line of Cain ends and passes into oblivion. The future under God lies elsewhere, in a new beginning. ✶

SETH – THE BEGINNING OF FAITH

Adam lay with his wife again. She bore a son, and 25 named him Seth,[a] 'for', she said, 'God has granted me another son in place of Abel, because Cain killed him.' Seth too had a son, whom he named Enosh. At that time 26 men began to invoke the LORD[b] by name.

✶ The hope expressed in 3: 20 finds its continuance not in the line of Cain which ends in ruthless arrogance, but in *another son* who replaces murdered Abel.

25. By a type of word play similar to that used to explain the name Cain (see p. 51) the son is called *Seth* because God

[a] *That is* Granted.
[b] *This represents the Hebrew consonants* YHWH, *probably pronounced* Yahweh, *but traditionally read as* Jehovah.

granted, Heb. *sath*, Eve this other son. In English we might say he is called Grant, because God granted him.

26. The family tree of Adam through Seth is to be developed at length in the priestly genealogy in chapter 5; here we are given only a fragment, tracing it as far as Seth's son *Enosh*. This the J narrator uses to explain the origin of the worship of God under the name YHWH (see p. 6).

Enosh: used in poetic passages, particularly in Job and Ps. as the equivalent to *'ādām*, meaning man.

'what is man (*'enōsh*) that thou shouldst remember him, mortal man (*'ādām*) that thou shouldst care for him?'
(Ps. 8: 4).

At that time men began to invoke the LORD (Heb. YHWH) *by name:* a statement which is not easy to reconcile with certain other Old Testament passages. The priestly tradition in Exod. 6: 3 links the name YHWH with the revelation first given to Moses at the exodus (cp. Exod. 3: 13f). Certainly the exodus experience provided the Hebrews with the all-important clue to the character of their God and hence to the meaning of his name.

'I am the LORD your God who brought you out of Egypt, out of the land of slavery' (Exod. 20: 2).

The J narrator, however, in line with his universalizing tendency, insists that the name YHWH was known long before the exodus; indeed it is part of Israel's pre-history. The origin and the meaning of the name YHWH are still a mystery to modern scholars. There may well have been different traditions in Israel as to when God was first worshipped as YHWH. For J it is inconceivable that the true God could ever have been anything other than YHWH. ✳

THE FAMILY TREE OF ADAM — FROM ADAM TO NOAH

This is the record of the descendants of Adam. On the 5
day when God created man he made him in the likeness
of God. He created them male and female, and on the 2
day when he created them, he blessed them and called
them man.

Adam was one hundred and thirty years old when he 3
begot a son in his likeness and image, and named him
Seth. After the birth of Seth he lived eight hundred years, 4
and had other sons and daughters. He lived nine hundred 5
and thirty years, and then he died.

Seth was one hundred and five years old when he 6
begot Enosh. After the birth of Enosh he lived eight 7
hundred and seven years, and had other sons and daughters. He lived nine hundred and twelve years, and then 8
he died.

Enosh was ninety years old when he begot Kenan. 9[a]
After the birth of Kenan he lived eight hundred and 10
fifteen years, and had other sons and daughters. He 11
lived nine hundred and five years, and then he died.

Kenan was seventy years old when he begot Mahalalel. 12
After the birth of Mahalalel he lived eight hundred and 13
forty years, and had other sons and daughters. He lived 14
nine hundred and ten years, and then he died.

Mahalalel was sixty-five years old when he begot 15
Jared. After the birth of Jared he lived eight hundred 16
and thirty years, and had other sons and daughters. He 17
lived eight hundred and ninety-five years, and then he
died.

[a] *Verses 9–32: cp. 1 Chr. 1: 2–4.*

18 Jared was one hundred and sixty-two years old when
19 he begot Enoch. After the birth of Enoch he lived eight
20 hundred years; and had other sons and daughters. He
    lived nine hundred and sixty-two years, and then he
    died.

21 Enoch was sixty-five years old when he begot Methu-
22 selah. After the birth of Methuselah, Enoch walked with
    God for three hundred years, and had other sons and
23 daughters. He lived three hundred and sixty-five years.
24 Having walked with God, Enoch was seen no more,
    because God had taken him away.

25 Methuselah was one hundred and eighty-seven years
26 old when he begot Lamech. After the birth of Lamech
    he lived for seven hundred and eighty-two years, and
27 had other sons and daughters. He lived nine hundred and
    sixty-nine years, and then he died.

28 Lamech was one hundred and eighty-two years old
29 when he begot a son. He named him Noah, saying,
    'This boy will bring us relief from our work, and from
    the hard labour that has come upon us because of the
30 LORD's curse upon the ground.' After the birth of Noah,
    he lived for five hundred and ninety-five years, and had
31 other sons and daughters. Lamech lived seven hundred
32 and seventy-seven years, and then he died. Noah was
    five hundred years old when he begot Shem, Ham and
    Japheth.

* This is the first in a series of family trees which the priestly
writer (P) uses to provide his narrative with a religious
historical framework. Others will be found in chapter 10
and 11: 10–32. Here he spans the period from creation to the

first major break in human history, the flood. A summary of
this family tree listing only the names is to be found in
1 Chron. 1: 1–4.

This *record of the descendants of Adam* (verse 1) is noteworthy
in two respects: (*a*) it contains ten names, (*b*) it attributes to
these pre-flood worthies abnormally long life spans. Enoch,
with three hundred and sixty-five years to his credit, dies
prematurely in comparison with the rest.

In both respects it is reminiscent of extra-biblical, ancient
near eastern material. One Babylonian tradition speaks of
ten kings, descended from heaven, who reigned before the
flood; while in the Sumerian king list eight kings rule prior
to the flood for 241,000 years. (The appropriate texts in
English translation will be conveniently found in the books
noted on p. 113.)

The contrasts between the biblical and the Mesopotamian
traditions are equally interesting. The Mesopotamian 'kings
descended from heaven' before the flood are semi-divine,
mythological figures; Gen. 5 claims to be speaking of mortal
men. It is in line with this that even the longest lived worthy
in Gen. 5, Methuselah, with nine hundred and sixty-nine
years to his credit, comes nowhere near the longevity attributed to his Mesopotamian counterparts.

There has been much speculation, but no certainty, concerning the life span attributed to the various descendants
of Adam. The figures differ significantly in the textual
traditions which have come down to us. The Hebrew text has
1,656 years from creation to the flood, the Samaritan text
1,307 years and the Septuagint 2,262. Nor is it clear whether
any religious significance should be read into the numbers.
It has been claimed that here we have evidence of the pristine
vitality of early man, a vitality which diminishes the further
we move from creation with man held ever more strongly in
the grip of evil. The numbers in this family tree, however,
hardly bear this out. Methuselah, the eighth in the list,
outlives all his predecessors, while Enoch who has the most

intimate relationship with God is the shortest lived. We must simply conclude that the Hebrews, like many other peoples, believed that abnormally long life spans should be attributed to the worthies who lived in the days before the flood.

1–2. The prologue to the family tree recalls the priestly account of the creation of man in Gen. 1: 26, 27 with slight variations in phrasing. Man is here said to have been *made in the likeness of God* (verse 1) instead of 'made in our image and likeness' (Gen. 1: 26). The language of the creation hymn is more closely echoed in verse 3 where Adam begets a son *in his likeness and image*, implying that the 'image and likeness' of God is common to all humanity, part of an inheritance passed on from Adam.

2. *and called them man*: an addition to the language of Gen. 1: 27, underlining the fact that *'ādām, man*, is a generic term, meaning mankind or humanity and including both male and female.

3–31. The family tree contains nine sections each conforming to a stereotyped pattern with the following common elements:

(i) a name of a person;

(ii) the age of the person at the time of the birth of his eldest son, thus marking the successive generations;

(iii) a note of the years the person lived after the birth of this eldest son and the fact that he had other sons and daughters, thus accounting for the population explosion which led to the whole earth being populated;

(iv) the age of the person at death.

This pattern is broken, or rather supplemented, at two points.

(*a*) Additional information is given concerning *Enoch*, the seventh name on the list. *Enoch walked with God* (verse 22) and *having walked with God, Enoch was seen no more, because God had taken him away* (verse 24). In Babylonian tradition the seventh king is Enmeduranna of Sippar, a town sacred to

Shamash the sun god. This Enmeduranna, highly favoured by the sun god, is initiated into the secrets of heaven and earth, taught the art of divination and becomes the originator of the Babylonian guild of diviner priests. Similar mythological speculation about Enoch was known in later Jewish tradition; it surfaces in the extra-biblical books of Enoch and Jubilees, and in the New Testament in Jude 14, 15. An echo of Babylonian speculation may survive in the number of years attributed to Enoch, three hundred and sixty-five, an appropriate life span for one associated with the sun god. But the priestly writer has firmly closed the door on much speculation. For him, the supreme honour is not esoteric knowledge or the gift of divination, but the life of faith, a life lived in intimate communion with God. This is what is meant by saying, *Enoch walked with God*, a phrase used again only in Gen. 6: 9 where the priestly writer uses it to describe Noah.

24. *Enoch was seen no more, because God had taken him away:* such a life of communion with God releases a man from the terror and power of death (cp. Ps. 49: 15; 73: 24). How this happened is not stated, but the same word 'take' is used in the mysterious story of Elijah's translation to heaven in 2 Kings 2: 1, 10.

(*b*) In verse 29 Lamech's son *Noah* becomes the focal point of hope. By a typical word play (see 4: 1 and 4: 25), the name *Noah* is explained as signifying one who will *bring . . . relief*, Heb. *niḥam*, from the curse which God pronounced upon the ground in 3: 17.

In the case of Noah, the tenth name in the list, the stereotyped pattern is left incomplete. We are only given his age at the time of the birth of three sons *Shem, Ham and Japheth*. The story of Noah is to be the theme of the following chapters. ✳

The flood and the tower of Babel

THE FLOOD – GENESIS 6–8

Stories of a catastrophic flood occur in the folklore of many peoples scattered across the world. Much of the material is conveniently collected together in J. G. Frazer's *Folklore in the Old Testament*, pp. 46–143. The stories differ widely, some of them having scant resemblance to the Genesis narrative. We have already noted evidence for such a flood tradition in the Ancient Near East, in the Sumerian and Babylonian king lists which draw a distinction between kings who ruled before and after the flood (see p. 61). The text of such Mesopotamian flood stories, in so far as they are extant, will be found in the books listed on p. 113. The Sumerian version has survived in very fragmentary form. In it the flood, sent by a decision of the gods, sweeps over the earth for seven days and seven nights. Only one man, king Ziusudra, who had been divinely forewarned of impending disaster, escapes through constructing a huge boat. The later Babylonian version survives remarkably complete in the xith Tablet of the epic of Gilgamesh. It provides interesting parallels to the Genesis story. Like Noah, Utnapishtim, his Babylonian counterpart, warned by the gods of the coming catastrophe, constructs a ship to take aboard with him not only his wife and family, but 'the seed of all living things'. The flood-carrying storm blows up with such ferocity that the gods themselves are terrified. When the storm abates Utnapishtim's ship grounds on the top of mount Nisir. He then uses the same kind of test as Noah to discover whether the waters are further abating.

> 'When the seventh day arrived
> I sent forth and set free a dove.

The dove went forth, but came back.
There was no resting place for it, she turned round.
Then I sent forth and set free a swallow.
The swallow went forth and came back.
There was no resting place for it and she turned round.
Then I sent forth and set free a raven.
The raven went forth and seeing that the waters had
    diminished,
He eats, circles, caws and turns not round.'

                              (cp. Gen. 8: 6–12.)

On disembarking from his ship Utnapishtim
        'offered a sacrifice.
I poured out a libation on the top of the mountain.

· ·

The gods smelled the savour,
the gods smelled the sweet savour,
the gods crowded like flies round the sacrificer.'

                              (cp. Gen. 8: 20–1).

The similarities in broad outline and in certain points of
detail between the Gilgamesh and the Genesis versions are
too striking to be accidental. Both probably derive from a
common older Mesopotamian tradition, fragments of which
are preserved in the Sumerian version. But if they share a
common origin the end product is very different.

What lies behind such flood stories? It is sometimes claimed,
particularly in popular books on the Bible, that there is firm
evidence, provided by archaeological investigation of sites
in southern Mesopotamia, to prove that the flood as recounted
in Genesis is a dateable, historical event. Certainly excava-
tions at sites such as Ur, Kish and Shuruppak have unearthed
evidence of severe flooding; but such flooding is of a more or
less local nature and occurs at different times at different sites.
In other words, archaeology provides us with no evidence
whatsoever to substantiate the Genesis story of a universal
flood in which 'the waters increased over the earth until they

covered all the high mountains everywhere under heaven. The waters increased and the mountains were covered to a depth of fifteen cubits' (22·5 ft, 6·9 m) (Gen. 7: 19–20).

It is important to recognize that the epic of Gilgamesh does not claim to be a historical document. It is an example of religious mythology; its theme a man's search for immortality. The whole of the flood story in Tablet XI is subservient to this major theme. It tells how Gilgamesh, in the course of his search, comes face to face with Utnapishtim, the one mortal who has come to share the immortality which rightly belongs to the gods alone. That the change from mortality to immortality should have been thought of as happening through surviving a catastrophic flood, is hardly surprising, since severe flooding was one of the recurring hazards of life in southern Mesopotamia. What we find in the epic of Gilgamesh is myth drawing upon typical events for its own purposes. As the flood is mythologized, it is embellished, reshaped and exaggerated until its link with any particular historical happening becomes more and more tenuous. Genesis 6–8 take the process one stage further. Here is the story of a flood which tradition has already mythologized, being re-mythologized, given new religious meaning in the light of Israel's faith.

Wherein lie the main differences between the Genesis story and its Mesopotamian parallel? It has been customary to speak of the superiority of the Genesis story in terms of 'its ethical spirit and its monotheistic conception of God'; and indeed in such terms Genesis 6–8 far outshine the Gilgamesh epic. In Gilgamesh no reason is given for the flood. It is introduced as a decision of the gods. Later, the blame for it is fixed firmly on one god Enlil who is said to have sent the deluge 'without reflection'. Another fragmentary version of the Mesopotamian flood tradition, the Atrahasis epic, does suggest a reason:

'The land became great, the people multiplied;
The land became sated(?) like cattle.

66

> The god (Enlil) heard their noise,
> And said to the great gods,
> "Great has become the noise of mankind,
> With their tumult they make sleep impossible".'

Even divine insomnia, however, can hardly be alleged as an adequate ethical reason for destroying humanity. In contrast, the prologue to the Genesis flood story in Gen. 6: 5–8 is ethically motivated throughout. Further, although the flood is a decision of the gods, the storm frightens the gods out of their wits. The goddess Ishtar, in violent distress, disclaims all responsibility for what has happened. The other gods weep with her:

> 'The gods all humbled sit and weep,
> Their lips drawn tight.'

When Utnapishtim offers his sacrifice of thanksgiving for deliverance:

> 'The gods crowded like flies round the sacrificer.'

To all of this, the restrained, dignified monotheism of the Genesis story stands in the sharpest contrast.

These contrasts, however, merely scratch the surface of the essential difference between the two traditions. It is not a question of superiority or inferiority. We are dealing with two different analyses of what is basic to man's religious experience. Utnapishtim, the man who achieves immortality, is replaced by a man who remains a man, a mortal man who in the fulness of time will die (Gen. 9: 29). The Genesis story is not obsessed by death or motivated by the quest for immortality; instead it directs our attention to the responsible relationship in which man stands to God and to the tragic consequences which may stem from such a relationship. In this context we hear sounded some of the dominant notes in the faith of Israel – judgement, salvation and covenant.

Although there are difficulties in detail in making a literary analysis of chapters 6–8, it is best to see the flood story in its present form as a blending of material from J and P. Some of the more obvious reasons for this have been mentioned on p. 4; a fuller discussion will be found in the larger commentaries noted on p. 113.

THE PROLOGUE TO THE FLOOD STORY, ACCORDING TO THE J TRADITION

6 When mankind began to increase and to spread all over
2 the earth and daughters were born to them, the sons of the gods saw that the daughters of men were beautiful; so they took for themselves such women as they chose.
3 But the LORD said, 'My life-giving spirit shall not remain in man for ever; he for his part is mortal flesh: he shall live for a hundred and twenty years.'
4 In those days,[a] when the sons of the gods had intercourse with the daughters of men and got children by them, the Nephilim[b] were on earth. They were the heroes of old, men of renown.
5 When the LORD saw that man had done much evil on earth and that his thoughts and inclinations were
6 always evil, he was sorry that he had made man on earth,
7 and he was grieved at heart. He said, 'This race of men whom I have created, I will wipe them off the face of the earth—man and beast, reptiles and birds. I am sorry that
8 I ever made them.' But Noah had won the LORD's favour.

* The J narrator introduces the flood story with a prologue which falls into two inter-related sections:

[a] *Prob. rdg.; Heb. adds* and also afterwards (*cp. Num. 13: 33*).
[b] *Or* giants.

(i) 6: 1–4, in which he uses for his own purposes a fragment of pagan mythology (see p. 7).

(ii) 6: 5–8, in which he provides us with his own commentary on the human situation.

1–4. This section is one of the strangest passages in the whole of the Old Testament. After noting, as the P tradition in chapter 5 had done, the rapid expansion in world population (verse 1), it declares in verse 2 *the sons of the gods saw that the daughters of men were beautiful: so they took for themselves such women as they chose:* and verse 4 speaks of the time when *the sons of the gods had intercourse with the daughters of men.*

From the time of the Aramaic Targums onwards, misplaced piety has led commentators to side-step the plain meaning of the text. Attempts have been made to explain *the sons of the gods* as nobility or royalty or the true worshippers of God. By all Old Testament analogy *the sons of the gods* can only mean one thing, divine beings. In Job 1: 6 and 2: 1 the same phrase is translated by the N.E.B. *the members of the court of heaven.* This meaning was recognized in early Jewish tradition in Jubilees 5: 1 and Enoch 6:2 and probably in the New Testament in 2 Peter 2: 4 and Jude 6. Further, *the daughters of men* cannot mean anything other than mortal women. Such stories of sexual intercourse between gods and mortal women are common enough in religious mythology. In Canaanite mythology, as it is known to us from the Ugaritic texts, El, the supreme god, seduces two women and begets the twin gods Dawn and Evening. Nor is it strange that such a story should be used to explain the existence on earth of a race of supermen, the *Nephilim* (verse 4). *Nephilim* is a word of very uncertain meaning. In Num. 13: 33, the only other Old Testament reference, the Nephilim are men of gigantic size who make the Hebrew incomers to Canaan feel 'no bigger than grasshoppers'. There may be an editorial reference to this Numbers' story in the phrase 'and also afterwards' which the N.E.B. has omitted after *In those days* at the beginning of verse 4 (see N.E.B. footnote).

Read on this level, the story would evoke neither surprise nor moral comment in many religious traditions. But the J narrator has his own way of dealing with what to him is a piece of pagan mythology. Into it he inserts a word of divine judgement in verse 3.

3. Both the text and the interpretation of this verse present serious difficulties. The difficulties centre on the meaning to be given to *My life-giving spirit* (Heb. my spirit) and to the verb translated *remain*. There are two main lines of interpretation reflected in the various English translations.

(i) 'My spirit' may be given an ethical sense and the verb translated 'strive' or 'rule' (see A.V.). This implies that there is a limit to God's patience. In the face of outrageous evil, God will withdraw his spirit and leave man to reap the tragic consequences. Linguistically this is a very dubious rendering.

(ii) N.E.B. takes spirit to mean the gift of life which comes to man from God (see Gen. 1: 2), and thus gives a translation which is part commentary *My life-giving spirit*. This gift of life is not man's inalienable possession; it will not *remain in man forever*. This is linguistically sounder and gives a better connection with what follows.

he shall live for a hundred and twenty years: this may mean that evil has now so corrupted man that, in comparison to the long-lived worthies of chapter 5, man's life span is to be restricted to one hundred and twenty years or it may indicate the strictly limited period that remains for humanity before it is overwhelmed in the judgement of the flood.

he for his part is mortal flesh: perhaps it is best to take *man* in this verse to refer to the strange, bastard race of semi-divine beings who are the fruit of the liaison between *the sons of the gods* and *the daughters of men*. Such creatures are not gods; they share the weakness of humanity, they are mortal flesh. They are doomed to die within one hundred and twenty years.

The narrator thus passes judgement on this fragment of pagan mythology. He sees in it only a tragic overstepping of

the boundary which separates God from man. It is the sign of
a deep-seated corruption infecting all life. Evil has a demonic
dimension which fully warrants God's stern reaction. Aptly,
the story becomes part of the preface to the flood.

5-8. The human scene, in the narrator's judgement, tells
the same tale. Man had *done much evil on earth*. This was but
the outward expression of the inner corruption of *his thoughts
and inclinations*, all the plans he devised in his mind.

6. *he was sorry that he had made man*: the evil in the heart of
man provokes a reaction in the heart of God. The problem
of how to translate the Heb. verb *niham*, 'he was sorry',
when applied to God is well illustrated in 1 Sam. 15 where it
occurs four times. Twice N.E.B. renders 'repent' (verses 11
and 35), twice 'changed his mind' (verse 29). The danger
in its use is underlined in 1 Sam. 15: 29 where it is stated that
God does not 'change his mind; he is not man that he should
change his mind'. God may not be man, subject to human
weakness and inconsistency, but, for the Old Testament, God
is nothing if not actively personal. There is no hesitation in
applying to God the most intensely personal and human
emotions. Better the dangers of personal language than an
impersonal blank.

he was grieved: only found here with reference to God. It
expresses the pain in God's heart. The related noun is used
of human travail in Gen. 3: 16, 17 and 5: 29 (see note on
3: 17).

7. In the midst of judgement on this *race of men* (Hebrew
'*ādām*) the word of hope is heard.

8. *Noah had won the LORD's favour*: no indication is given
as to why Noah is so favoured. The text does not imply that
Noah *won*, in the sense of 'earned', *the LORD's favour*.
J is content to point to, and to leave unexplained, the LORD's
gracious attitude to Noah. *

THE PROLOGUE TO THE FLOOD ACCORDING
TO THE P TRADITION

9 This is the story of Noah. Noah was a righteous man,
the one blameless man of his time; he walked with God.
10,11 He had three sons, Shem, Ham and Japheth. Now God
saw that the whole world was corrupt[a] and full of
12 violence. In his sight the world had become corrupted,
13 for all men had lived corrupt lives on earth. God said to
Noah, 'The loathsomeness[b] of all mankind has become
plain to me, for through them the earth is full of violence.
I intend to destroy them, and the earth with them.'

✱ 9. *This is the story of Noah:* see note on 2: 4.
The description of Noah as *a righteous man, the one blameless
man of his time,* does not necessarily mean that Noah was a
paragon of virtue, devoid of any moral flaws. The word
righteous has a legal background in the Old Testament: it
indicates someone who is 'in the right' in the eyes of accepted
social custom or in his relationships with others. *blameless* is
most commonly found in the language of worship to denote
a sacrifice 'without blemish' and therefore acceptable as an
offering to God (see Exod. 12: 5). What makes Noah 'in the
right' and 'acceptable' is the fact that like Enoch *he walked
with God:* see note on 5: 22.
11–13. As in the case of the J prologue in 6: 1–8, the
necessity for judgement is traced to the cancer of evil, described
in the words *violence* or lawlessness. English translations,
including N.E.B., miss something of the inner logic of these
verses. The Hebrew words translated *corrupt* (verse 11),
corrupted and *corrupt* (verse 12) come from the same root as
destroy (verse 13). The world God intends to destroy has

[a] *Or* ripe for destruction.
[b] *Or* end.

already destroyed itself through violence. It is ripe for destruction: see N.E.B. footnote.

13. *The loathsomeness of all mankind:* although *loathsomeness* is a possible translation, giving reasonable sense, it is perhaps better to read with N.E.B. footnote and most other English versions 'the end', the word which is used in prophetic teaching to describe God's irrevocable judgement on a sinful community; see Amos 8: 2. 'The end' is in sight. The writing is clearly on the wall. *

THE FLOOD—GOD COMMANDS NOAH TO MAKE THE ARK (P)

'Make yourself an ark with ribs of cypress; cover it with 14 reeds and coat it inside and out with pitch. This is to be its 15 plan: the length of the ark shall be three hundred cubits, its breadth fifty cubits, and its height thirty cubits. You 16 shall make a roof for the ark, giving it a fall of one cubit when complete; and put a door in the side of the ark, and build three decks, upper, middle, and lower. I intend to 17 bring the waters of the flood over the earth to destroy every human being under heaven that has the spirit of life; everything on earth shall perish. But with you 18 I will make a covenant, and you shall go into the ark, you and your sons, your wife and your sons' wives with you. And you shall bring living creatures of every kind 19 into the ark to keep them alive with you, two of each kind, a male and a female; two of every kind of bird, 20 beast, and reptile, shall come to you to be kept alive. See 21 that you take and store every kind of food that can be eaten; this shall be food for you and for them.' Exactly as 22 God had commanded him, so Noah did.

✻ The description of the construction of the ark is far from clear at many points. This may be seen by comparing N.E.B. with other English versions, particularly in verses 14 and 16.

14. *an ark:* Heb. *tēbāh*, only found in this narrative and in the story of the infant Moses for whom, according to Exod. 2: 3, his mother makes a 'basket'. (A totally different word is used in Hebrew when the reference is to the 'ark' as a symbol of God's presence in the midst of his people, see 1 Sam. 4: 1ff.) It is certainly not a usual word for a boat or ship. It may be an Egyptian loan word in Hebrew. In both narratives it indicates some kind of floating object which God provides to save the life of a man who is called to serve God's purposes.

ribs of cypress: the type of wood is uncertain. Some English versions simply transliterate the Hebrew word *gopher*.

cover it with reeds: instead of *reeds*, the traditional Hebrew text has 'rooms', literally 'nests' (see R.S.V.). An alteration to the vowels in the text gives the meaning *reeds* which are used to bind the frame together. In Exod. 2: 3 Moses' basket is made of rushes. The reeds are then caulked with *pitch*, Heb. *kōper*, a word only found here in the Old Testament, and probably related to the Akkadian *kupru* which Utnapishtim uses for a similar purpose in the construction of his ship. The ancient Egyptians made very sea-worthy boats out of reeds as Thor Heyerdahl has demonstrated with his Egyptian modelled boat *Ra II*.

15. On the assumption that a *cubit* is approximately eighteen inches, Noah's floating home is some four hundred and fifty feet long, seventy-five feet broad and forty-five feet high ($137 \times 22 \cdot 8 \times 13 \cdot 7$ m). It has been calculated that its displacement would be over forty thousand tons (about 40 million kgm). No doubt Noah would need every inch of space. He was building a floating zoo (see verses 19, 20) as well as a floating hotel.

16. *roof:* seems a preferable translation to 'window' (A.V.) or 'light' (R.V.), although it is far from certain.

giving it a fall of one cubit when complete: this is little more than a guess at the meaning of an extremely confusing Hebrew phrase. Presumably it seeks to convey the picture of a gently sloping roof. It is also possible to translate 'Make a sky light for the ark, terminating it within a cubit from the top' (E. A. Speiser in the Anchor Bible commentary, see 'A note on further reading' p. 113). It is difficult, however, to see why there should be reference to a sky light and none to a roof.

17. *the waters of the flood:* outside this narrative the word *flood*, Heb. *mabbūl*, is only found in Ps. 29: 1 'The LORD is king above the flood', a reference to God's sovereignty over the primeval waters of chaos. From the description of the flood in 7: 11 it is clear that P thinks of the flood in terms of the breakdown of creation, a cosmic catastrophe in which the waters which had been gathered at creation above the vault of heaven and the waters of the great abyss broke loose to overwhelm the world: see note on Gen. 1: 16.

18. *But with you I will make a covenant:* for the first time the word *covenant* appears in Genesis. What this covenant means is not unfolded until 9: 8–11. In general, a *covenant* (Heb. *berīt*) is an agreement which binds two parties to one another (see Gen. 31: 44). When in the Old Testament covenant is used in a theological context, the initiative in establishing the covenant relationship always comes from God.

19. *two of each kind:* contrast the J tradition in 7: 2. For P, the distinction which J makes between clean and unclean animals does not exist in Israel until much later when at Sinai God gave Israel the law, including all the regulations which were to govern the way in which the community worshipped and offered sacrifice (see Exod. 20ff).

22. Noah shows his trust in God by obedience (cp. Heb. 11: 7). Abram is later to show the same mark of faith; he 'set out as the LORD had bidden him' (12: 4).   *

THE COMMAND TO GO INTO THE ARK (J)

7 The LORD said to Noah, 'Go into the ark, you and all
your household; for I have seen that you alone are
2 righteous before me in this generation. Take with you
seven pairs, male and female, of all beasts that are ritually
clean, and one pair, male and female, of all beasts that
3 are not clean; also seven pairs, male and female, of every
4 bird—to ensure that life continues on earth. In seven days'
time I will send rain over the earth for forty days and
forty nights, and I will wipe off the face of the earth
5 every living thing that I have made.' Noah did all that
the LORD had commanded him.

* This section is in many respects the J parallel to 6: 14–22.
It has its own distinctive vocabulary and ideas. Instead of
'your sons, your wife and your sons' wives' (6: 18), it speaks
of *your household* (7: 1). Instead of 'two of each kind' of all
living creatures (6: 19), it speaks of *seven pairs ... of all
beasts that are ritually clean, and one pair ... of all beasts that are
not clean* (7: 2); see the note on 6: 19. Instead of a breakdown
of cosmic order as the waters of the flood are unleashed, it
speaks merely of *forty days and forty nights* of rain (7: 4).

   It describes Noah in a phrase which partly recalls 6: 9,
you alone are righteous before me in this generation (7: 1). It ends,
like the previous section, by pointing to Noah's obedient
trust: *Noah did all that the LORD had commanded him* (7: 5). *

THE FLOOD

6 He was six hundred years old when the waters of the
flood came upon the earth.
7   And so, to escape the waters of the flood, Noah went

into the ark with his sons, his wife, and his sons' wives. And into the ark with Noah went one pair, male and 8–9 female, of all beasts, clean and unclean, of birds and of everything that crawls on the ground, two by two, as God had commanded. Towards the end of seven days 10 the waters of the flood came upon the earth. In the year 11 when Noah was six hundred years old, on the seventeenth day of the second month, on that very day, all the springs of the great abyss broke through, the windows of the sky were opened, and rain fell on the earth for forty days 12 and forty nights. On that very day Noah entered the ark 13 with his sons, Shem, Ham and Japheth, his own wife, and his three sons' wives. *a*Wild animals of every kind, 14 cattle of every kind, reptiles of every kind that move upon the ground, and birds of every kind*b*—all came to Noah 15 in the ark, two by two of all creatures that had life*c* in them. Those which came were one male and one female 16 of all living things; they came in as God had commanded Noah, and the LORD closed the door on him. The flood 17 continued upon the earth for forty days, and the waters swelled and lifted up the ark so that it rose high above the ground. They swelled and increased over the earth, and 18 the ark floated on the surface of the waters. More and 19 more the waters increased over the earth until they covered all the high mountains everywhere under heaven. The 20 waters increased and the mountains were covered to a depth of fifteen cubits. Every living creature that moves 21 on earth perished, birds, cattle, wild animals, all reptiles, and all mankind. Everything died that had the breath of 22

[a] *So Sept.; Heb. prefixes* They.
[b] *So Sept.; Heb. adds* every winged bird.   [c] *Lit.* spirit of life.

23 life[a] in its nostrils, everything on dry land. God wiped out every living thing that existed on earth, man and beast, reptile and bird; they were all wiped out over the whole earth, and only Noah and his company in the ark survived.

✳ The description of the flood comes in the main from the P tradition, but embedded into it are fragments of what must once have been the parallel J version. This is particularly noticeable in verses 8 and 9, where we find reference to *clean and unclean*. Indeed in verse 9 several ancient versions read 'the LORD' instead of *God*. In verse 12 J's *forty days and forty nights* of rain has been combined with P's description of the breakdown of cosmic order. At the end of verse 16, it is said that *the LORD* closed the door on Noah.

6. *He was six hundred years old*: better, 'Now Noah was six hundred years old'. This sentence marks the beginning of the section which recounts the coming of the flood, rather than the end of the previous section as printed in the N.E.B. In terms of P's chronology this means that the flood came one hundred years after the birth of Noah's three sons, Shem, Ham and Japheth; see 5: 32. Six hundred years is one of the basic time units in Babylonian tradition.

11. *on the seventeenth day of the second month*: such precise dating is characteristic of P, cp. 8: 4, 13, 14. The Septuagint reads 'on the twenty-seventh day of the second month', thus making the period from the coming of the flood to the day when the whole earth was again dry, exactly one year; see 8: 14. In the Hebrew text the period is one year and ten days.

14. N.E.B. omission of 'they' at the beginning of the verse (see footnote) is hardly necessary. It may be translated 'together with'. Its omission in Septuagint may be purely a question of translation. The same holds true for the end of the

[a] *So Sept.; Heb.* breath of the spirit of life.

verse where Heb., though undoubtedly repetitive, is not impossible.

15. *all creatures that had life in them:* as N.E.B. footnote makes clear, *life* in Heb. is exactly the same phrase which in 6: 17 is applied to human beings and translated 'the spirit of life'. It indicates that all life has its source in God's creativity; it is his gift.

16. *and the LORD closed the door on him:* a graphically naïve expression which draws attention to the LORD's care for Noah even in the midst of catastrophic judgement.

19. This verse does not necessarily imply a universal flood; *all the high mountains everywhere under heaven* are simply the highest points of the world as known to the narrator. Similarly Gen. 41: 57 says that, during a period of severe but local famine in the Ancient Near East, 'The whole world came to Egypt to buy corn from Joseph'.

21–3. The totality of destruction reverberates in the repeated *every* and *all* of these verses; they are the same word in Hebrew:

Every living creature . . . all reptiles and all mankind (verse 21);
Everything died . . . everything on dry land (verse 22);
God wiped out every living thing . . . they were all wiped out (verse 23).

In striking relief is the one exception, in whom are to be concentrated all God's promises and all hope for a future beyond disaster, *only Noah and his company in the ark survived.*

22. *the breath of life in its nostrils:* lit. 'the breath of the spirit of life in its nostrils' (see N.E.B. footnote). The Hebrew seems to be a combination of 'the breath of life' of 2: 7, and 'the spirit of life' of 6: 17; 7: 15. Perhaps the phrases have been deliberately combined to intensify their meaning. Everything in which there was the faintest glimmer of life, died.

23. *God wiped out:* Heb. 'and he wiped out', the subject being left to be understood from context, as frequently in Hebrew. This seems better than taking the verb as a passive and translating 'everything was wiped out' (cp. A.V.). ✻

THE FLOOD RECEDES (P)

24 When the waters had increased over the earth for a
8 hundred and fifty days, God thought of Noah and all the
wild animals and the cattle with him in the ark, and he
made a wind pass over the earth, and the waters began to
2 subside. The springs of the abyss were stopped up, and so
were the windows of the sky; the downpour from the
3 skies was checked. The water gradually receded from the
earth, and by the end of a hundred and fifty days it had
4 disappeared. On the seventeenth day of the seventh month
5 the ark grounded on a mountain in Ararat. The water
continued to recede until the tenth month, and on the
first day of the tenth month the tops of the mountains
could be seen.

* The first glimpse into the heart of God in the flood story
revealed the painful inevitability of judgement (7: 7 'he was
grieved at heart'), the second, in the midst of judgement,
speaks of the mystery of God's continuing care.

8: 1 f. *God thought of Noah:* lit. God remembered Noah.
Such 'remembering' by God in the Old Testament is not
merely the recalling of the past, but the spring-board for his
present outgoing activity. In Gen. 30: 22 God's thinking of,
remembering, Rachel means answering her prayers by grant-
ing her a child (cp. Gen. 19: 29). Here God acts to re-establish
order out of chaos.

he made a wind to pass over the earth: see note on Gen. 1: 2.
'Wind' rather than 'spirit' is the correct translation here;
but the reference in verse 2 to the *abyss* and the *windows of the
sky* (or heaven) recalls the cosmology in the opening verses
of the creation hymn in Gen. 1. What takes place is a new
creation, another conquest of the watery powers of chaos, a

new creation in which God's concern reaches out not only to Noah, but to *all the wild animals and the cattle with him in the ark*.

3. The translation of this verse is misleading. In Hebrew 'recede' is a different word from that translated 'recede' in verse 5. The 'recede' of verse 5 comes from the same Hebrew root translated *disappeared*; *it had disappeared* is not a very meaningful translation. The water did not disappear off the earth until later; see verse 13. The picture which should be conveyed is that of the water gradually receding until *by the end of one hundred and fifty days* it had so 'subsided' or 'diminished' that the ark came to rest on a mountain top.

4. *On the seventeenth day:* as in 7: 11 the Septuagint reads 'the twenty seventh day'.

a mountain in Ararat: lit. the mountains of Ararat. Ararat is a mountainous region north of lake Van in what is now Armenia. The region was known in Assyrian documents as Urartu. Within this range there is one peak, called Ararat, some seventeen thousand feet high. This distant northern range, towering above the northern limits of the fertile crescent, may well have been the highest mountains known to the Hebrews and therefore a suitable point for the grounding of the ark. The Gilgamesh epic grounds Utnapishtim on Mt Nisir further south and east. ✳

THE EARTH BECOMES HABITABLE (J)

After forty days Noah opened the trap-door that he 6 had made in the ark, and released a raven to see whether 7 the water had subsided,*ᵃ* but the bird continued flying to and fro until the water on the earth had dried up. Noah waited for seven days,*ᵇ* and then he released a dove 8 from the ark to see whether the water on the earth had

[a] to see . . . subsided: so Sept.; Heb. om.
[b] Noah . . . days: prob. rdg., cp. verse 10; Heb. om.

9 subsided further. But the dove found no place where she could settle, and so she came back to him in the ark, because there was water over the whole surface of the earth. Noah stretched out his hand, caught her and took

10 her into the ark. He waited another seven days and again

11 released the dove from the ark. She came back to him towards evening with a newly plucked olive leaf in her beak. Then Noah knew for certain that the water on the

12 earth had subsided still further. He waited yet another seven days and released the dove, but she never came back.

13 And so it came about that, on the first day of the first month of his six hundred and first year, the water had dried up on the earth, and Noah removed the hatch and looked out of the ark. The surface of the ground was dry.

* It was a common practice among navigators in the ancient world to release birds to see whether dry land was near. As we have seen, pp. 64–5, Noah's sending forth of the birds has a close parallel in the Gilgamesh epic. The Genesis version, however, has a more lively human interest. Notice the way in which Noah reaches out his hand to bring the dove back into the ark (verse 9). Think of the relief, the excitement, the hopes we are invited to share as the dove comes back a second time with *a newly plucked olive leaf in her beak* (verse 11).

6. *Noah opened the trap-door:* as other English versions indicate, the word translated *trap-door* is usually rendered 'window' and that is how N.E.B. renders it elsewhere, see Gen. 26: 8; 2 Kings 9: 30. The word, however, simply means an opening.

to see whether the waters had subsided: not in Heb. The addition of this phrase, following Septuagint, clarifies the meaning of the passage, but is not strictly necessary. The addition is the only justification for adding *further* to the end of the same phrase in verse 8.

8. *Noah waited for seven days:* the only justification for this addition to the text – it appears in none of the versions – is the *another seven days* of verse 10. The narrative makes perfectly good sense without the addition. Noah releases a raven, then, after an unspecified time, a dove. Once the dove returns with the olive leaf, Noah waits seven more days and sends forth the dove again.

13. *on the first day of the first month of his six hundred and first year:* New Year's day would be a fitting day for Noah to discover that *the water had dried up on the earth.* It was at the New Year festival that the triumph of order over the powers of chaos, represented by the unruly waters, was celebrated and re-experienced by the community; see p. 13.

The time factor in this verse is difficult to reconcile with the statement in the following verse that it was not until *the twenty-seventh day of the second month* that the whole earth was dry. The J and P traditions seem to work with different chronologies of the flood. For J the flood period amounts in all to sixty-one days; forty days and nights of rain, followed by the twenty-one days during which Noah sends forth the birds before he steps on dry land (7: 4; 8: 6–13). For P the flood lasts in all for one year and ten days according to Heb., exactly one year according to Septuagint, although it is unclear whether a solar or a lunar year is intended. There have been many attempts to account for and to explain the religious significance of the detailed chronological data in P, but none is very convincing. By the longer period which he assigns to the flood and by the cosmological language in which it is described, P is stressing the theological importance of the flood. It marks the major break in the story of humanity. ✳

83

DISEMBARKATION (P)

14 By the twenty-seventh day of the second month the
15,16 whole earth was dry. And God said to Noah, 'Come out
of the ark, you and your wife, your sons and their wives.
17 Bring out every living creature that is with you, live
things of every kind, bird and beast and every reptile that
moves on the ground, and let them swarm over the earth
18 and be fruitful and increase there.' So Noah came out
19 with his sons, his wife, and his sons' wives. Every wild
animal, all cattle, every bird, and every reptile that moves
on the ground,*ᵃ* came out of the ark by families.

✲ For P the disappearance of the flood waters marks the
beginning of a new era in which the original order of creation
is confirmed and modified. In this first scene from the new
era the continuity with the original order of creation is
stressed. God's original purpose for every living creature *be
fruitful and increase* is reasserted (see note on Gen. 1: 22).
But the new era cannot simply be a re-run of the old, or it
too will lead to a watery grave. The problem of man and the
disturbance which he brings into the natural order is to be the
theme of the second scene in 9: 1–17.

19. The Septuagint reading, followed by the text, seems
here preferable. At the point of disembarkation we expect
mention of the fourfold classification of living creatures other
than man, wild animals, cattle, birds and reptiles as in 7: 21. ✲

THE PROMISE (J)

20 Then Noah built an altar to the LORD. He took ritually
clean beasts and birds of every kind, and offered whole-

[a] all cattle . . . ground: *so Sept.; Heb.* every reptile and every bird,
everything that moves on the ground.

offerings on the altar. When the LORD smelt the soothing 21
odour, he said within himself, 'Never again will I
curse the ground because of man, however evil his
inclinations may be from his youth upwards. I will
never again kill every living creature, as I have just
done.

> While the earth lasts   22
> seedtime and harvest, cold and heat,
> summer and winter, day and night,
> shall never cease.'

* As in the Gilgamesh epic, so in the J tradition the story of
the sending forth of the birds is immediately followed, after
disembarkation, by the offering of a sacrifice.

20. *an altar:* for the first time in the Genesis narrative
specific mention is made of *an altar*, although the sacrifices
offered by Cain and Abel in Gen. 4: 3–4 probably presuppose
an altar. Altars of various kinds are known in the Old Testament. They range all the way from somewhat primitive
earth or stone structures to the bronze and gold altars which
graced Solomon's temple (1 Kings 7: 48; 8: 64). Whatever
its design, the altar remained the place where man made his
approach to God through sacrifice.

ritually clean beasts and birds: for the first time, one reason
for the division of beasts and birds into 'clean' and 'unclean'
becomes clear. Only the *ritually clean* may be offered to God.
The same distinction was used to differentiate between what
was regarded as fit and unfit for human consumption; see the
lists in Lev. 11 and Deut. 14: 1–21.

offered whole-offerings: the reason for Noah's offering is not
explicitly stated. Sacrifices in the Old Testament are of many
different kinds and expressive of many different religious
needs and aspirations. The *whole-offerings* are a type of sacrifice
in which the animal or bird is burned in its entirety on the
altar and thus goes up to God – the Heb. for whole-offering is

'*ōlāh* from a verb meaning 'to go up'. The ritual, as it was practised in Israel, is described in Lev. 1. The whole-offering is a gift to God. It may express joy, gratitude or dedication. Gratitude for having survived disaster seems the most likely explanation of Noah's *whole-offerings*.

the LORD smelt the soothing odour: although the *soothing odour* becomes a recognized technical expression in the context of Israel's sacrificial worship (see Lev. 1: 9 ff.) to describe a sacrifice acceptable to God, nowhere else in the Old Testament do we find *the LORD smelt the soothing odour*. It immediately recalls the Gilgamesh epic where

'The gods smelled the savour
The gods smelled the sweet savour' (see p. 65).

Whatever this language may be intended to convey in the Gilgamesh epic, we must remember the limitations which surround words like *the LORD smelt* in the Old Testament (see note on 6: 7). Similarly *soothing odour* is a misleading translation if it conveys the idea of something which placates God's anger or soothes his ruffled feelings. The whole phrase is a vividly anthropomorphic way of saying that the LORD found Noah's sacrifice acceptable.

21. *he said within himself:* lit. 'said in his heart'. The J flood tradition ends where it began (6: 7) in the heart of God. The 'I will wipe them off the face of the earth' of 6: 7 is answered by a twofold *never again*. This 'never again' is rooted in the recognition by God of a fact. However evil man may have become, the answer to the problem of man does not lie in total destruction, richly deserved though it may be.

22. In the heart of God there is a mystery of patience of which the unchanging rhythm of the seasons,

> *seedtime and harvest, cold and heat,*
> *summer and winter,*

and the constant succession of *day and night* is the token. Here is the God who 'makes his sun rise on good and bad alike

86

and sends the rain on the honest and the dishonest' (Matt. 5: 45).

In the J flood story we move from tragedy through judgement to hope. This for the narrator is the continuing reality of man under God. ✳

THE NEW AGE (P)

God blessed Noah and his sons and said to them, 'Be **9** fruitful and increase, and fill the earth. The fear and dread 2 of you shall fall upon all wild animals on earth, on all birds of heaven, on everything that moves upon the ground and all fish in the sea; they are given into your hands. Every creature that lives and moves shall be food 3 for you; I give you them all, as once I gave you all green plants. But you must not eat the flesh with the life, which 4 is the blood, still in it. And further, for your life-blood 5 I will demand satisfaction; from every animal I will require it, and from a man also I will require satisfaction for the death of his fellow-man.

> He that sheds the blood of a man,   6
> for that man his blood shall be shed;
> for in the image of God
> has God made man.

But you must be fruitful and increase, swarm throughout 7 the earth and rule*a* over it.'

✳ As we have already seen (see note on 8: 14), a new age begins for P after the flood. It is the age in which man now lives. The lines of continuity with the old are clearly marked. The original blessing given to man in the creation hymn (see

[a] *Prob. rdg.*, *cp. 1: 28*; *Heb.* increase.

note on 1: 28) is reaffirmed, '*Be fruitful and increase, and fill the earth.*' But the new is not the old. The original verdict on all creation 'very good' (1: 31) is no longer heard. The harmony of creation has been shattered.

2. Man who rebels against God, man who murders a brother, now slaughters other living creatures. The animals and birds who once came to man to be named, now flee from him in *fear and dread*.

3. this assumes that man was originally vegetarian. Once his food was *all green plants*; this is an imprecise reference back to 1: 29 where 'green plants' are the food for creatures other than man, and man is given seed-bearing 'plants' like grain and fruit-bearing trees. Now *every creature that lives and moves shall be food for you*.

4–6. But if man now kills other living creatures for food, it must be forcibly brought home to him that his lordship is not absolute. It is hedged around by two restrictions.

(i) Although man may eat other living creatures, he must not eat *flesh with the life, which is the blood, still in it* (verse 4). In the traditions of many peoples, blood, for understandable reasons, is equated with life. Often as life departs, or a person's vitality is undermined by serious injury, blood flows from the body. In some societies this leads to the drinking of blood as a means of achieving greater vitality; in other societies it leads to blood being considered taboo, prohibited from any ordinary usage. For the Old Testament, life, Heb. *nepesh*, comes as a gift from God (see note on 2: 7). At death it returns to God. It is, therefore, not under man's control. In the sacrificial ritual, the blood equated with life is always offered to God on the altar, and it is the blood which opens up the possibility of new life when the relationship between God and man has been disturbed by human sinfulness (see Lev. 17: 10–14). The restriction on eating *flesh with the life, which is the blood, still in it* is designed to remind man that life, even in the animal world, is not at his free disposal. Later this restriction became the basis of the Jewish dietary law which allows the orthodox Jew to eat only 'kosher' meat from which the blood has been drained.

(ii) *And further* (verse 5) what applies to man's relationship to other living creatures, applies even more to his relationship to his fellow man. A man's *life-blood* is under God's peculiar protection:

(*a*) from attack by animals, *from every animal I will require it.* 'When an ox gores a man or a woman to death, the ox shall be stoned' (Exod. 21: 18);

(*b*) from attack by his fellow man. The penalty for murder is death. Here the narrator quotes in verse 6 what may be a piece of ancient sacral law, memorable by its terseness and its rhythmic form. Only six Hebrew words lie behind the first two lines of the English text of verse 6. A more literal rendering would be,

> The shedder/ of blood/ of man/
> by man/ his blood/ shall be shed/.

for that man, because of the murder committed; most English translations render 'by man', man having the responsibility for exacting the death penalty. Both translations are linguistically possible.

In the case of man it is not simply the fact that life is God's gift which guarantees its sanctity; an additional theological reason is given, that peculiar relationship to God which is indicated in the creation hymn by *the image of God* (see note on 1: 26–7). What verse 6 does not say is as clear an indication of its character as what it does say. It does not attempt to legislate or to stipulate a definite pattern of law and order for society. It does not say how, or precisely by whom, the death penalty is to be enacted. It seeks solely to enunciate a fundamental religious principle, the sanctity of human life. Paradoxically, it protects the sanctity of human life by demanding the taking of life.

7. N.E.B. makes this verse a virtual quotation of 1: 28 by altering the final verb in the sentence from 'increase' to *rule*

(see footnote). The alteration is plausible; 'increase' and 'rule' are very similar in Hebrew. The second 'increase' in the sentence may be an accidental repetition of the first. On the other hand, once the limitation on man's freedom has been stressed, verse 7 may be no more than a return to the blessing theme of verse 1 with 'increase' deliberately repeated for the sake of emphasis. ✻

THE COVENANT WITH NOAH

8, 9 God spoke to Noah and to his sons with him: 'I now make my covenant with you and with your descendants
10 after you, and with every creature that is with you, all birds and cattle, all the wild animals with you on earth,
11 all that have come out of the ark.*a* I will make my covenant with you: never again shall all living creatures be destroyed by the waters of the flood, never again shall there be a flood to lay waste the earth.'

12 God said, 'This is the sign of the covenant which I establish between myself and you and every living creature with you, to endless generations:

13　　　My bow I set in the cloud,
　　　　sign of the covenant
　　　　between myself and earth.
14　　　When I cloud the sky over the earth,
　　　　the bow shall be seen in the cloud.

15 Then will I remember the covenant which I have made between myself and you and living things of every kind. Never again shall the waters become a flood to destroy
16 all living creatures. The bow shall be in the cloud; when

[a] So Sept.; Heb. adds to all wild animals on earth.

I see it, it will remind me of the everlasting covenant between God and living things on earth of every kind.' God said to Noah, 'This is the sign of the covenant which 17 I make between myself and all that lives on earth.'

✽ 8–17. These verses are the P parallel to the promise theme contained in the J tradition in 8: 14–22. Twice we hear God's *never again* (verses 11, 15; cp. 8: 21). But the promise is here set within the framework of one of the key theological ideas of the P tradition, *the covenant* (see note on 6: 18). There are certain distinctive features in the covenant described in this section.

(i) It is a covenant which is comprehensive in its scope and breadth; not merely a covenant between God and Noah, but between God and Noah, his *descendants* and *every living creature, all birds and cattle, all the wild animals with you on earth* (verse 10). The final phrase in verse 10 in the Hebrew text 'to all the wild animals on earth', which N.E.B., following Septuagint, omits (see footnote) may be a scribe's way of drawing attention to this fact; yes, notice, he says, it applies even to them.

(ii) It is an *everlasting covenant* (verse 16), which is established to *endless generations* (verse 12) – the same Hebrew word lies behind 'everlasting' and 'endless'. This is a covenant permanent in its validity at every point in time across the entire history of Israel's experience. It is not merely a past event, which happened once to Noah after the flood, but an ever present reality to faith (cp. 17: 7, 13, 19).

(iii) It is a covenant which is authenticated by a sign (verses 12, 13, 17). A 'sign' (Heb. *'ōt*) for the Old Testament, when used in a religious context, may either be some thing or some happening which is mysterious or inexplicable – witness the strange events which happened in Egypt prior to and accompanying the exodus, 'signs and portents' as Deuteronomy calls them (Deut. 6: 22; 7: 19) – or it may be some thing or happening which in itself is quite ordinary or commonplace, such as circumcision (Gen. 17: 11) or the sabbath (Exod. 31: 13, 17). Whatever its character, it becomes a sign because it points beyond itself to some aspect of God's nature or activity. Here, as the *sign of the covenant* God sets *the bow . . . in the cloud* (verses 13, 14, 16), the rainbow. The rainbow finds a place in the religious mythology of many peoples. Sometimes it is regarded as the bow which the warrior or storm god lays aside in the sky after he has defeated his enemies. The Old Testament can speak of God 'stringing the bow' and 'preparing his deadly shafts' (Ps. 7: 12; cp. Hab. 3: 9). Perhaps the Hebrews were familiar with such an explanation of the rainbow. But such is not its meaning here. The rainbow is now *sign of the covenant*. What does this mean? The rainbow is pointing not to the bare fact of the covenant, but to that which lies behind it, the utter dependability of God. With almost childlike naïvety P makes the bow a sign not simply for man, but for God to see, *when I see it, it will remind me of the everlasting covenant* (verse 16). The rainbow is the assurance that God will never forget his promise never again to destroy the earth.

(iv) If a covenant binds two parties together in common loyalty or interest, the initiative which brings the covenant into being usually comes from one of the parties. Throughout this section emphasis is repeatedly laid on God's initiative. This is *my covenant with you* (verse 11) . . . *the covenant which I establish between myself and you* (verse 12) . . . *the covenant which I have made* (verse 15; cp. 17). The other party to the covenant is mere spectator. Even Noah promises nothing and no demands are laid upon him.

Thus, in terms of the covenant, P speaks his own word of hope after the flood, hope founded entirely upon God's dependability and God's initiative. For later Judaism the covenant with Noah was of fundamental significance. It applied to all men, and from it were derived seven basic precepts binding upon all humanity, see A. Cohen, *Everyman's Talmud* p. 65. *

THE SONS OF NOAH

The sons of Noah who came out of the ark were 18
Shem, Ham and Japheth; Ham was the father of Canaan.
These three were the sons of Noah, and their descendants 19
spread over the whole earth.

Noah, a man of the soil, began the planting of vine- 20
yards. He drank some of the wine, became drunk and lay 21
naked inside his tent. When Ham, father of Canaan, saw 22
his father naked, he told his two brothers outside. So 23
Shem and Japheth took a cloak, put it on their shoulders
and walked backwards, and so covered their father's
naked body; their faces were turned the other way, so
that they did not see their father naked. When Noah 24
woke from his drunken sleep, he learnt what his youngest
son had done to him and said: 25

> 'Cursed be Canaan,
> slave of slaves
> shall he be to his brothers.'

And he continued: 26

> 'Bless, O LORD,
> the tents of Shem;*a*
> may Canaan be his slave.
> May God extend*b* Japheth's bounds, 27
> let him dwell in the tents of Shem,
> may Canaan be their slave.'

After the flood Noah lived for three hundred and fifty 28
years, and he was nine hundred and fifty years old when 29
he died.

[a] Bless . . . Shem: *prob. rdg.; Heb.* Blessed is the LORD the God of Shem.
[b] *Heb.* japht.

✻ It has been well said that this passage is 'filled with difficulties and obscurities for which the final word has not been spoken'. Part of the trouble may be that, as in the case of 6: 1–4, the J narrator is himself trying to clear a path through what for him is very strange territory. There are many byways in which it is possible to linger and get lost.

Noah, in this section, lying *drunk and . . . naked* (verse 21) is a very different character from the Noah of the flood 'righteous and blameless who walked with God' (6: 9). Whenever *the sons of Noah* have been mentioned previously, they have been referred to as Shem, Ham, and Japheth (5: 32; 6: 10), presumably in the order of their birth; and this is the order in which they appear in the heading to this section in verse 18. In verse 24, however, Ham is described as the *youngest son*. Some versions, seeing the difficulty, translate 'the younger son', but this is not possible linguistically. Further, when we come to the curse and blessing in verses 25–7, Shem and Japheth remain but Ham disappears to be replaced by Canaan who is mentioned in each of the three verses. The sentence *Ham was the father of Canaan* (verse 18, cp. 22) is probably the narrator's way of preparing us for this change. All this is evidence of the uneasy way in which this section fits into its present context in Genesis.

If we regard the section as a fragment of an ancient tradition which was once totally unrelated to the story of the flood, we move into the realm of pure speculation (see p. 50); if we ask what it may mean within the context of J's narrative a variety of different approaches are possible.

An *ethical* approach reads the narrative as typical, a warning of the unfortunate consequences of over-indulgence in the produce of the vine, an over-indulgence to which even a good man may yield.

As a *cultural myth* or *inventor saga* the narrative explains the origin of the cultivation of the vine. In this approach any ethical judgement on Noah is wholly inappropriate; he is but learning the potency inherent in his new discovery. The

94

translation *Noah, a man of the soil, began the planting of vineyards* (verse 20) adds support to this approach although the Hebrew construction is far from clear. It is characteristic that an invention which in certain other cultures is attributed to a god, for example Dionysus in ancient Greece, is in the Old Testament attributed to a man (see note on 4: 20–2). It is appropriate that the man should be Noah who in the flood tradition has links with Armenia from which the vine seems to have spread into the ancient near east.

The section may also be regarded as the fulfilment of the prophecy in 5: 29 with its word play on the name Noah (see comment on 5: 29). Noah, by cultivating the vine, provides man with the palliative for the burdensome life of toil to which he was condemned by God. There may be elements of truth in all these approaches but they seem to represent the byways rather than the main path. There is little doubt that the key to the whole must be found in verses 25–7 where Canaan, Shem and Japheth are not to be taken primarily as individuals but as representatives of the peoples who spring from them. It was common practice in the ancient world for communities and tribal groups to trace their ancestry back to what is called an eponymous ancestor, an ancestor who gave his name to the group. Thus the Greeks or Hellenes traced their history back to Hellen, the Dorians, to Dorus. Not only was the name of a people traced back to such an eponymous figure, but the fortunes and characteristics of the people were reflected in the stories about him. If we combine this with the concepts of the curse and blessing in the Old Testament (see notes on 1: 20–3 and 3: 14–15) we can understand how a curse or blessing pronounced on Canaan, Shem and Japheth was considered to live on and work itself out in the lives of their descendants, thus accounting for the character and fortunes of the peoples who sprang from them.

25. The Curse on Canaan. Canaan is condemned to be *slave of slaves*, a Hebrew idiom meaning the most menial of slaves, cp. Song of Songs, the best song. This reflects not only

the conquest of Canaan by the Hebrews, but when linked to the shameless conduct of Ham in verse 22, signifies the strong revulsion which Hebrew faith felt against Canaanite religion with its fertility cult involving sexual practices such as ritual prostitution (see note on 2: 15–17). The curse may be read as both condemnation and warning since Canaanite religion continued to exercise a powerful fascination for many Hebrews up to the time of the exile to Babylon in the sixth century B.C. Deuteronomy contains repeated warnings against the practices of the indigenous peoples of Canaan who will 'draw your sons from the LORD and make them worship other gods' (Deut. 7: 4).

26. *Bless, O LORD, the tents of Shem*: this translation presupposes an emendation to the traditional Hebrew text, as does the R.S.V. 'Blessed by the LORD my God be Shem', although in this latter case it is merely a change in the vowels added to the text. N.E.B. footnote gives the Hebrew text 'Blessed is the LORD the God of Shem'. The main argument against this reading is that we expect in this verse a blessing on Shem, corresponding to the curse on Canaan in verse 25 and the blessing on Japheth in verse 27. This could hardly be expressed by 'Blessed be the LORD' which is an invitation to praise God. Yet the Hebrew text has much to commend it. It is supported by all the ancient versions and in context makes good sense. If in the curse on Canaan we see the revulsion of the Hebrews from the degradation of Canaanite religion, then the true blessing which came to Israel – of whom Shem is the remote ancestor (see 10: 21–31; 11: 27–32) – was her faith, her relationship with the LORD. Only in so far as Israel continued to bless the LORD did she herself have any continuing blessing. 'Blessed be the LORD' echoes across liturgical texts in the Old Testament (Gen. 24: 27; Exod. 18: 10; Ps. 28: 6), sometimes in the form 'Blessed be the LORD, the God of Israel' (Ps. 41: 13). In favour of the N.E.B. text, it may be argued that the familiar liturgical cry has early replaced the original text. 'Bless, O LORD, the tents of Shem' is then a plea that the

descendants of Shem will experience all the fulness and richness of life which is implied in a divine blessing.

27. *May God extend Japheth's bounds:* again a typical play on
similar sounding words in Hebrew. The Hebrew verb translated *extend . . . bounds* is *japht.*

let him dwell in the tents of Shem: this seems to imply a
situation in which Japheth was acting in alliance with or in
association with Shem in conquering the Canaanites or in
keeping them in subjection. There has been much inconclusive
speculation about the identity of Japheth. Historically the
Philistines are obvious candidates since they were doing their
own conquest of Canaan from the Mediterranean sea-board
as the Hebrews were attempting to consolidate their infiltra-
tion from the east. The Hittites have also been proposed. In
the Table of the Nations, however, in chapter 10 the Philistines and the Hittites are not among the descendants of
Japheth; they are descendants of Ham (see 10: 14, 15). This
is not an insuperable objection since we cannot be sure the
principle of classifying peoples here is the same as in chapter 10
(see p. 101). The difficulty of finding historical circumstances
in Israel's life to correspond to this verse has led some Christian
commentators to see in the verse a prophecy of the gathering
of both Jews and Gentiles into the Christian church, the 'sons
of Japheth' in 10: 2-5 being in the main non-Semitic speaking
peoples of the Aegean region and thus a suitable symbol of the
non-Jewish world. Apart from the inherent improbability
in this interpretation, it makes no sense of the concluding
statement *may Canaan be their slave.*

In principle, an interpretation of these verses which sees
human history as the outworking of God's purposes in terms
of curse and blessing is correct, although the precise detail
may be obscure.

28-9. The story of Noah is here rounded off by P. He
completes the information about Noah which he had left
unfinished at 5: 32, noting, as in the case of all the other
worthies in chapter 5, his age at death. *

THE ROLL CALL OF THE NATIONS

10 These are the descendants of the sons of Noah, Shem, Ham and Japheth, the sons born to them after the flood.

2[a] The sons of Japheth: Gomer, Magog, Madai, Javan,[b]
3 Tubal, Meshech and Tiras. The sons of Gomer: Ash-
4 kenaz, Riphath and Togarmah. The sons of Javan:
5 Elishah, Tarshish, Kittim[c] and Rodanim.[d] From these the peoples of the coasts and islands separated into their own countries, each with their own language, family by family, nation by nation.

6[e] The sons of Ham: Cush, Mizraim,[f] Put and Canaan.
7 The sons of Cush: Seba, Havilah, Sabtah, Raamah and
8 Sabtecha. The sons of Raamah: Sheba and Dedan. Cush was the father of Nimrod, who began to show himself
9 a man of might on earth; and he was a mighty hunter before the LORD, as the saying goes, 'Like Nimrod, a
10 mighty hunter before the LORD.' His kingdom in the beginning consisted of Babel, Erech, and Accad, all of
11 them in the land of Shinar. From that land he migrated
12 to Asshur and built Nineveh, Rehoboth-Ir, Calah, and
13[g] Resen, a great city between Nineveh and Calah. From Mizraim sprang the Lydians, Anamites, Lehabites,
14 Naphtuhites, Pathrusites, Casluhites, and the Caphtorites,[h] from whom the Philistines were descended.

15   Canaan was the father of Sidon, who was his eldest

[a] *Verses 2–4: cp. 1 Chr. 1: 5–7.*
[b] *Or* Greece.   [c] *Or* Tarshish of the Kittians.
[d] *So Sam.; Heb.* Dodanim.   [e] *Verses 6–8: cp. 1 Chr. 1: 8–10.*
[f] *Or* Egypt.   [g] *Verses 13–18: cp. 1 Chr. 1: 11–16.*
[h] and the Caphtorites: *transposed from end of verse; cp. Amos 9: 7.*

son, and Heth,[a] the Jebusites, the Amorites, the Girga- 16
shites, the Hivites, the Arkites, the Sinites, the Arvadites, 17, 18
the Zemarites, and the Hamathites. Later the Canaanites
spread, and then the Canaanite border ran from Sidon 19
towards Gerar all the way to Gaza; then all the way to
Sodom and Gomorrah, Admah and Zeboyim as far as
Lasha. These were the sons of Ham, by families and 20
languages with their countries and nations.

Sons were born also to Shem, elder brother of Japheth, 21
the ancestor of all the sons of Eber. The sons of Shem: 22[b]
Elam, Asshur, Arphaxad, Lud[c] and Aram. The sons of 23
Aram: Uz, Hul, Gether and Mash. Arphaxad was the 24
father of Shelah, and Shelah the father of Eber. Eber 25
had two sons: one was named Peleg,[d] because in his time
the earth was divided; and his brother's name was
Joktan. Joktan was the father of Almodad, Sheleph, 26
Hazarmoth, Jerah, Hadoram, Uzal, Diklah, Obal, 27, 28
Abimael, Sheba, Ophir, Havilah and Jobab. All these 29
were sons of Joktan. They lived in the eastern hill- 30
country, from Mesha all the way to Sephar. These were 31
the sons of Shem, by families and languages with their
countries and nations.

These were the families of the sons of Noah according 32
to their genealogies, nation by nation; and from them
came the separate nations on earth after the flood.

* To understand this roll call of the nations, an abbreviated
form of which is to be found in 1 Chron. 1: 4–23, we must
look backwards and forwards. Here is the fulfilment of the

[a] Or the Hittites.   [b] *Verses 22–29: cp. 1 Chr. 1: 17–23.*
[c] Or the Lydians.   [d] *That is* Division.

command to Noah after the flood, 'Be fruitful and increase and fill the earth' (9: 1). It witnesses to the vitality of the blessing given to Noah. From this one man all the nations of the world are derived. Under God, *the separate nations on earth* are one community; all come from *the families of the sons of Noah* (verse 32). But the roll call also looks forward. Here the movement is from the many to the one. While in the introductory verse the sons of Noah are cited as *Shem, Ham and Japheth*, their descendants are cited in the reverse order, *the sons of Japheth* in verses 2–5, *the sons of Ham* in verses 6–20 and *the sons of Shem* in verses 21–31. It is as if three roads lead from Noah out into the world. Two of them, those of the sons of Japheth and the sons of Ham, turn into cul-de-sacs from the religious standpoint. They are dealt with first. The third, that of the sons of Shem, is the road which, along one of its branches (see verse 24), travels on into the history of Israel to become the way of the people of God. Politically Israel is but one, and not a very significant one, among the many nations in God's world; theologically for the Old Testament, she is the one in whose faith the hopes of all are carried.

The framework of this section comes from P, but into it there has been incorporated some material from the J tradition, particularly in verses 8–9 and 24–30. The names in the list vary in type. Some are personal names, those of the eponymous ancestors of various races (see note on 9: 25–7); some are plural in form, Kittim, Rodanim, verse 4, and the names of those descended from Mizraim (Egypt) in verses 13 and 14; while the names in verses 16–18 have in Hebrew an ending which indicates nationality, the Jebusites, the Amorites, etc. Increasing knowledge of the world of the Ancient Near East has shed light on most of the names in the list, but some are still obscure. A detailed discussion of the individual names will be found in the larger commentaries by S. R. Driver and J. Skinner (see p. 113) and more recently in an article in the *Interpreter's Dictionary of the Bible* Vol. III, pp. 235 ff.

We shall comment only on names which occur frequently elsewhere in the old Testament or in cases where N.E.B. suggests a different rendering from earlier English translations.

The classification of the nations into three groups has not been done on scientifically definable racial or linguistic grounds. The principle of classification seems to be broadly geographic, with historical and political factors modifying the picture at certain points. The fact that in some cases the same names appear differently classified – in verse 7 Havilah and Sheba are among the sons of Ham, while in verse 27 they are among the sons of Shem – may be due to the historical movement of peoples or it may reflect different traditions lying behind this roll call. In the main the sons of Japheth, verses 2–5, represent peoples to the north and west running in an arc from the Caspian sea to the Aegean; the sons of Ham, verses 6–20, extend from Phoenicia southwards into Africa and take in some of the tribal groups on the Asiatic side of the Red Sea; the sons of Shem, verses 21–3, begin in the east in the Iranian mountains and extend westwards into Mesopotamia and down into the Arabian peninsula.

2. *Javan:* here and in the parallel passage in 1 Chron. 1: 7 Septuagint renders 'Ionians', one branch of the ancient Greeks. Normally elsewhere in the Old Testament Septuagint renders 'Greeks' or 'Greece' (see N.E.B. footnote). In Dan. 8: 21 the kingdom of Javan is the empire of Alexander the Great.

4. *Tarshish:* appears elsewhere in the Old Testament as a trading port. It has been variously identified, for example, with Tartessus in Spain or with a town in Sardinia. N.E.B. footnote, by ignoring the traditional punctuation marks in Heb., reads 'Tarshish of the Kittians (Heb. *Kittim*)'. Since Kittim is identifiable with Kition, modern Larnaka in Cyprus, this suggests another Tarshish in the Aegean area which would be appropriate here. In Isa. 23: 1 ff both Tarshish and Kittim are Phoenician trading colonies.

Rodanim: is the reading of Heb. in 1 Chron. 1: 7 and of Samaritan and Septuagint here. In this case the reference is to the people of Rhodes, an island like many others in the Aegean area early colonized by the Phoenicians. The traditional Hebrew reading 'Dodanim' may be the result of the easy confusion between the letters 'r' and 'd' in Hebrew. The confusion could, however, just as easily have been the opposite way: Dodanim being a reference to the Dardanians of Asia Minor.

6. *Cush:* closely associated here with *Mizraim* (Egypt) and *Put* (Libya) must refer, as in Ezek. 29: 10, to the area south of Egypt namely Ethiopia. In this sense N.E.B. variously renders Cush (Isa. 20: 3 ff) or Nubia (Isa. 43: 3; 45: 4; Ps. 87: 4). Cush also, however, in the Old Testament refers to a people in Mesopotamia, the Kussites or Kassites. It is in this latter sense that Cush appears in verse 8 as the *father of Nimrod,* an ancient worthy associated with some of the major city states of the Tigris–Euphrates valley.

8f. *Like Nimrod a mighty hunter before the LORD:* just as biblical names have come down to us embedded in proverbial sayings – we speak, for example of someone having 'the patience of Job' – so the Hebrews knew of a proverbial saying in which the name of an ancient non-Hebrew hero Nimrod appeared. The identity of Nimrod has led to much speculation. On the assumption that he is a historical and not a purely legendary figure, there is much to be said for identifying him with Tukulti Ninurta I, thirteenth century B.C., the first Assyrian conqueror of Babylon. Such compound names of Assyrian kings sometimes appear in abbreviated form in the Old Testament; in 2 Kings 15: 19 Tiglath Pileser appears as Pul. The fondness of Assyrian kings for hunting is well documented in Assyrian records.

before the LORD: may mean either 'in the LORD's presence' or 'in the LORD's estimation'. Since the phrase is part of a traditional proverbial saying it is doubtful whether we can be certain of its precise meaning.

began to show himself a man of might: whoever he was, Nimrod was remembered as the first man to grasp at real power, 'a man of might', the first totalitarian figure.

10. *His kingdom in the beginning:* or 'the mainstay of his kingdom', his power base. The traditional Hebrew text then lists four centres of his power, Babel, Erech, Accad and Calneh. The existence of a city called Calneh in this area, however, is doubtful. A slight change in the vowels of the Hebrew text gives the reading *all of them* instead of Calneh.

Babel: see note on 11: 9.

in the land of Shinar: Shinar is the Hebrew equivalent of the Accadian Sumer, the region lying to the south of Babylon.

14. *the Caphtorites, from whom the Philistines were descended:* the justification for this reordering of the words at the end of the verse (see footnote) is that elsewhere in the Old Testament (Amos 9: 7; Jer. 47: 4) the Philistines are said to come from Caphtor, probably Crete. The traditional text makes the Philistines descendants of the Casluhites, but of this there is no evidence elsewhere. The Philistines were part of the wave of 'sea peoples' who, in the unsettled times of the late thirteenth and early twelfth centuries B.C., moved from their Aegean homeland, attacked Egypt and settled on the coastal plain of Canaan.

25. *one was named Peleg, because in his time the earth was divided:* a typical word play, the name *Peleg* having a similarity in sound to the verb translated *was divided* (see footnote where 'Division' is suggested for Peleg). What lies behind the cryptic remark that *in his time the earth was divided* is uncertain. Does it refer forward to the story of the Tower of Babel with its subsequent division of the human family into racial groups speaking different languages (see 11: 7 ff)? Heb. *peleg*, however, occurs in the Old Testament, for example in Isa. 32: 2, as a noun meaning either a natural water channel or an artifically constructed canal. Is the reference then to the time when men first began to build water channels, thus dividing the land?

Peleg is one of the two sons of *Eber*, the eponymous ancestor of the Hebrews, '*ibrī*. The roll call of the nations ends by tracing the descendants of the other brother *Joktan* into various tribal groups of the Arabian peninsula (verses 26–30). They form one of the cul-de-sacs among the sons of Shem. The story of the sons of Shem, through the line of Eber and Peleg, is to be continued in the family tree in II: 10 till it issues in Abram, the pilgrim forefather of the Hebrews. ✶

THE TOWER OF BABEL (J)

Once upon a time all the world spoke a single language **11** and used the same*a* words. As men journeyed in the 2 east, they came upon a plain in the land of Shinar and settled there. They said to one another, 'Come, let us 3 make bricks and bake them hard'; they used bricks for stone and bitumen for mortar. 'Come,' they said, 'let 4 us build ourselves a city and a tower with its top in the heavens, and make a name for ourselves; or we shall be dispersed all over the earth.' Then the LORD came down 5 to see the city and tower which mortal men had built, and 6 he said, 'Here they are, one people with a single language, and now they have started to do this; henceforward nothing they have a mind to do will be beyond their reach. Come, let us go down there and confuse their 7 speech, so that they will not understand what they say to one another.' So the LORD dispersed them from there 8 all over the earth, and they left off building the city. That is why it is called Babel,*b* because the LORD there 9 made a babble of the language of all the world; from that place the LORD scattered men all over the face of the earth.

[a] *Or* used few. [b] *That is* Babylon.

✻ The Babylonian setting of this story is unmistakable. It takes place *in the land of Shinar* (verse 2, see note on 10: 10). The city is named *Babel* (verse 9), Babylon. The materials used in the building of the tower are the characteristic *bricks and bitumen* (verse 3) of Mesopotamia, not stone which was readily available and used in Canaan. Behind *the tower with its top in the heavens* (verse 4) we glimpse the multi-storeyed temple towers, the 'ziggurats' of the Mesopotamian city states. Nabopolassar, king of Babylon (625–605 B.C.), describes the restoration work which he carried out on the ziggurat Etemenanki, 'house of the foundations of heaven and earth', in the following terms:

> 'The Lord Marduk commanded me concerning Etemenanki, the staged tower of Babylon, which before my time had become dilapidated and ruinous, that I should make its foundations secure in the nether world and make its summit like the heavens. I caused baked bricks to be made. As it were rains from on high which are measureless or great torrents, I caused streams of bitumen to be brought by the canal Arahtu.'

But if the raw materials of the story are Babylonian, J uses them to construct his own distinctive message. While there are aetiological elements in the story – the explanation of the name Babel given in verse 9, the answer to the question 'Why do men speak different languages?' in verses 7 and 9 – the real thrust of the story must be found elsewhere. It is best understood when we set what we are told about this tower against what we know of the ziggurats of Mesopotamia. The ziggurats were the cathedrals of the ancient near east, expressions of man's piety. They symbolized the bond between heaven and earth, the gods and man. The tower of Gen. 11: 1–9 is a godless edifice, the expression of man's desire for personal aggrandizement, *let us make a name for ourselves* (verse 4). Man unites in the anthem 'Glory to man in the highest' and the outcome is division and confusion. In the fear which prompts this action *or we shall be dispersed all over the earth* (verse 4) there is symbolized man's feverish search for security apart from God, a search doomed to failure. All mankind may belong in God's purposes to the one family of nations (see chapter 10), but this is now a broken, scattered family.

1. *Once upon a time:* this translation draws attention to the fact that there is no chronological relationship between the story of the tower and the roll call of the nations in chapter 10. The roll call of the nations has already recognized differences of language between peoples (see 10: 5, 20, 31); the story of the tower begins by noting that there had once been a single language, and seeks to give an explanation as to why this is no longer so.

spoke a single language and used the same words: lit. one language and one words. Heb. uses the plural form of 'one' as an adjective with 'words'. It seems best to take this as a parallel to the 'one language', hence *the same words*. Sometimes, however, the plural form of 'one' in Hebrew is used meaning 'a few'. In Gen. 27: 44 'one days' is translated 'for a while' in the N.E.B. (A.V. a few days). Hence the footnote 'used few words', a possible rendering but not so appropriate in context.

7. Note the reiterated '*Come*' or more colloquially 'come on'. Twice this 'come' has been on the lips of men. '*Come, let us make bricks . . .*' (verse 3); '*Come, . . . let us build ourselves a city*' (verse 4). Here this human 'come' is echoed by the LORD. What man does always evokes a response from God. As in Gen. 3, God's response to human pride and arrogance is the response of judgement.

let us go down: see note on 1: 26.

9. *That is why it is called Babel, because the LORD there made a babble:* this translation catches the word play which is there in the Hebrew. For the same reason verse 7 might well have been translated 'Come, let us go down there and make a babble of their speech'. In Accadian *babilu* (Babel) means

'the gate of god'; here the name is linked, quite unscientifically, with the Hebrew *balal* which means to confuse or confound. *

THE RELIGIOUS TEACHING OF GENESIS I–II

With the tower of Babel 'story myth' we hear the final chords in the series of symphonic variations on the theme of God and man which make up the prologue to the book of Genesis. A great composer builds upon a musical heritage, using motifs and themes from the past, yet transmuting them into his own distinctive idiom and style. He cannot be understood apart from his musical heritage; nor can he be fully explained by it. The Genesis narrators likewise, particularly J, draw upon a common stock of religious ideas from the world of the ancient near east, yet they present us with material which is distinctively their own.

Against the background of the wonder of creation by a transcendent God who is the source of all life and whose purposes in creation are good, there reverberates a sombre, tragic theme. Man, who has been made for God and made to exercise power responsibly under God, seeks to overstep the limits of his creatureliness. He attempts to place himself at the centre of existence and to find his own security. Chaos and insecurity, enmity between man and his brother ensue, God's judgement is an ever-present reality. But into this sombre theme there breaks again and again the note of hope. Rebellious man is never utterly rejected by God. Upon Cain the murderer is placed a protecting mark. When the world is overwhelmed by the flood disaster, one man 'wins the LORD's favour'. There is a covenant; there is a bow in the sky. This note of hope is the echo of Israel's experience as a nation from the moment when in the call of Abram, the pilgrim forefather, she believed herself to be the object of God's initiative and God's concern.

The tower of Babel story ends with men divided from one

another by barriers of language and *scattered . . . all over the face of the earth* (11: 9), the same narrator looks in faith to Abram and speaks of all nations finding a new unity in him:

> 'All the families on earth
> will pray to be blessed as you are blessed.'
>
> (Gen. 12: 3.)

That is why the prologue is linked to the rest of Genesis by a family tree which leads to Abram.

THE FAMILY TREE FROM SHEM TO ABRAM

10[a] This is the table of the descendants of Shem. Shem was a hundred years old when he begot Arphaxad, two 11 years after the flood. After the birth of Arphaxad he lived five hundred years, and had other sons and daugh- 12 ters. Arphaxad was thirty-five years old when he begot 13 Shelah. After the birth of Shelah he lived four hundred and three years, and had other sons and daughters.

14,15 Shelah was thirty years old when he begot Eber. After the birth of Eber he lived four hundred and three years, and had other sons and daughters.

16 Eber was thirty-four years old when he begot Peleg. 17 After the birth of Peleg he lived four hundred and thirty years, and had other sons and daughters.

18,19 Peleg was thirty years old when he begot Reu. After the birth of Reu he lived two hundred and nine years, and had other sons and daughters.

20 Reu was thirty-two years old when he begot Serug. 21 After the birth of Serug he lived two hundred and seven years, and had other sons and daughters.

[a] *Verses 10–26: cp. 1 Chr. 1: 24–27.*

Serug was thirty years old when he begot Nahor. 22
After the birth of Nahor he lived two hundred years, 23
and had other sons and daughters.

Nahor was twenty-nine years old when he begot 24
Terah. After the birth of Terah he lived a hundred and 25
nineteen years, and had other sons and daughters.

Terah was seventy years old when he begot Abram, 26
Nahor and Haran.

This is the table of the descendants of Terah. Terah 27
was the father of Abram, Nahor and Haran. Haran was
the father of Lot. Haran died in the presence of his father 28
in the land of his birth, Ur of the Chaldees. Abram and 29
Nahor married wives; Abram's wife was called Sarai,
and Nahor's Milcah. She was Haran's daughter; and he
was also the father of Milcah and of Iscah. Sarai was bar- 30
ren; she had no child. Terah took his son Abram, his 31
grandson Lot the son of Haran, and his daughter-in-law
Sarai Abram's wife, and they set out from Ur of the
Chaldees for the land of Canaan. But when they reached
Harran, they settled there. Terah was two hundred and 32
five[a] years old when he died in Harran.

* This is the second of the P tradition's family trees. In many
respects it recalls chapter 5. In chapter 5 Noah, whose story
was to be told in the following chapters, was the tenth name
in the list; here Abram who is to be the subject of the following chapters is the tenth name in the list. As in the case of
chapter 5, the ages attributed to these *descendants of Shem*
(verse 10) vary considerably in the major ancient versions.
From the flood to the birth of Abram is two hundred and
ninety years in the Hebrew text, one thousand and seventy

[a] *Or, with Sam.*, one hundred and forty-five.

in the Septuagint, and nine hundred and forty in the Samaritan tradition. One thing, however, is noticeable. In comparison with chapter 5 the average life span, particularly in the Hebrew text, has dropped considerably, and with it the age at which the eldest son is born. We are beginning to approach the level of normal life expectancy in the patriarchal narratives. Unlike chapter 5 there is no final sentence summing up, in the case of each person, his life span; in each case the Samaritan text adds such a sentence, while the Septuagint is content to add the final words of such a sentence, 'and he died', cp. chapter 5.

Many of the names which appear in the list are documented from extrabiblical sources, such as the Mari texts, as place names in north-west Mesopotamia, the region called Aram-naharaim in Gen. 24: 10, Aram of the two rivers, the Tigris and the Euphrates. Harran (verse 31) was an important trading centre in this area. Among other names known to us are Sarug (Serug, verses 20, 22), Nahur (Nahor, verses 23–5), Turahi (Terah, verses 24 ff) and Phaliga (Peleg, verses 16–18). Further information about the texts from Mari and from Nuzi (see verse 27) will be found in *The Making of the Old Testament* pp. 8 ff. Old Testament tradition elsewhere links the patriarchs with this general area and with the early Aramaean peoples whose presence in the area is amply vouched for in the first half of the second millennium B.C. Abram's descendants were to begin their confession of faith at harvest thanksgiving with the words 'My father was a homeless Aramaean' (Deut. 26: 5; cp. Gen. 28–9). Such strong links with north-west Mesopotamia added to the fact that in Gen. 12: 5 Harran is the point of departure of Abram's pilgrimage, has led many scholars to suspect the authenticity of the reference to *Ur of the Chaldees* (Heb. *Kasdim*) in verses 28 and 31 and in 15: 7. Of the importance of Ur there is no doubt; it was one of the major city states of southern Mesopotamia from the fourth millennium B.C. It lies, however, well outwith the region of Aram-naharaim, well to the south, near to what is now the head of the Persian gulf. There is, however, nothing improbable in a family or tribal group moving up the Tigris–Euphrates valley from Ur to Harran. The cities have this much in common; they were both important centres of the worship of the moon god. The reference to the *Chaldees* or *Kasdim* is certainly an anachronism in the time of Abram, since there is no evidence for the presence of people called Kasdim in southern Mesopotamia till near the end of the second millennium B.C. which is centuries later than the most likely period for Abram. It would not, however, be an anachronism from the point of view of the writer of this family tree.

27. *the descendants of Terah:* with the family of Terah we are on the threshold of Israel's religious pilgrimage. Of his sons, two are briefly mentioned since they are of no religious significance to the Old Testament.

Haran, the father of Lot, dies in Ur (verse 28). The initial letter in his name is different in Hebrew from the initial letter in the place name Harran (verse 31). English translations do not usually differentiate between the names; N.E.B. has done so by giving the place name a double 'r'.

Nahor (verse 29) marries his deceased brother's daughter. This was probably a type of marriage which was both legal adoption and marriage, a custom known to us from the texts from Nuzi in the middle of the second millennium B.C., texts which have provided us with many interesting social and legal practices which have links with the patriarchal narratives (see *The Making of the Old Testament* p. 10).

The future lies with Terah's other son *Abram*.

30. Briefly and without comment there is mentioned a fact which is the basis of much of the dramatic tension in the subsequent story of Abram. His wife *Sarai was barren; she had no child.* This is the harsh reality which seems to conflict with the promise that God is to make to Abram that he will become 'a great nation' (12: 2).

32. *Terah was two hundred and five years old when he died:*

this causes a difficulty. If, as seems likely, Abram was Terah's eldest son, born when Terah was seventy (verse 26), and if, according to 12: 5, he was seventy-five when he left Harran, he must have left his father's home sixty years before Terah's death. Since, however, the call to Abram is recounted at the beginning of chapter 12 immediately after the statement about Terah's death, it seems more natural to assume that Abram left home after his father's death, and this is explicitly stated in Stephen's speech in Acts 7: 4. The Samaritan text solves the problem neatly, perhaps too neatly, by reducing Terah's life span to one hundred and forty-five years (see footnote).

But Terah's death is more than a chronological puzzle. It is the end of a period in which the passing of time has been marked mainly by family trees which give us the briefest and most formal of information about many people. With Abram, we stand on the threshold of the patriarchal period. It is rich in characters of real human interest who know joy and sorrow, disappointment and success, and who find themselves held, as surely in their failings as in their piety, by the mystery of God's purposes.

A NOTE ON FURTHER READING

A fuller and more detailed commentary on Genesis 1–11 will be found in the stimulating commentary by G. von Rad, *Genesis* (S.C.M. Old Testament Library 1961). The Anchor Bible commentary on *Genesis* (Doubleday & Co. 1966) by E. A. Speiser provides a fresh translation, an excellent introduction to the problem of the literary sources, and sets the material within its wider cultural background. There is still much of value in the older commentaries by S. R. Driver (*Westminster Commentary* 12th ed. 1926) and by J. Skinner (*International Critical Commentary* 1910). Among the shorter commentaries, of particular value is that by N. M. Sarna, *Understanding Genesis* (The Heritage of Biblical Israel 1964); useful also are G. Henton Davies in *The Broadman Bible Commentary* Vol. 1 (Marshall, Morgan and Scott 1970), D. Kidner, *Tyndale Old Testament Commentary* 1969, C. T. Fritsch, *The Layman's Bible Commentary* 1963 and S. H. Hooke, *In the Beginning* (Clarendon Bible, Oxford University Press 1947).

We are fortunate that much of the comparative material essential for an understanding of Genesis 1–11 is readily available in English. J. G. Frazer, *Folklore in the Old Testament* (Macmillan & Co. 1923) collects a wealth of material, but the conclusions drawn from it are often dubious. The most complete and valuable collection of comparative material is *Ancient Near Eastern Texts relating to the Old Testament* ed. J. B. Pritchard (Princeton University Press 3rd ed. 1969). A briefer selection of texts with commentary will be found in *Documents from Old Testament Times* ed. D. Winton Thomas (Nelson & Sons 1958).

INDEX

Abel 50–1
  explanation of name 51
Abimelech 4
Abram 109–12
Adam 11, 28, 47
  family tree of 57–8, 59–63
'ādām (man) 23, 28, 31, 58, 62
'adāmāh (ground) 31
Adonai 6
altar 51, 85
Anu 14
Apsu 14–15
Ararat 81
ark 74
Aramaeans 110
Aram-naharaim 110
Asherah 26

Baal 11, 14, 26
Babel 10, 105–7
  explanation of name 106–7
bārā' (create) 15
Bereshith 2–3
berīt (covenant) 75
blessing, on man in creation 22
  renewed after flood 87–8
  Israel's faith as 96
blood 88–9
  equated with life 88
blood revenge 50–1
breath of life 31, 79

Cain, explanation of name 51
Cain
  and Abel 50–1
  builder of a city 56
  curse on 53–4
  family tree of 55–7
  mark of 54
Canaan
  curse on 95–6
  religion of 14–15, 96
Caphtorites 103

Chaldees 111
cherubim 48
covenant 75, 91–2, 107
creation
  and chaos 15
  and history 13
  goodness of 17
  six days of 17–27
  Babylonian myth 13
creation narratives 3–4, 12–28, 28–31
curse 45–6, 53, 95
Cush 32
  two fold identity 102

day, in creation hymn 18
death 46
Decalogue 27
demon 51
demūt (likeness) 25
Deuteronomy
  literary background 5
  religious teaching of 96
Dionysus 95
documentary hypothesis 6–7

'E' source 5–7
Ea 14
earth 20
  curse on 45
Eber 104
'ēd (flood) 30
Eden, garden
  location of 32–3
  mythological character of 33
El 33, 69
'elōhīm (gods or God) 40
Enmeduranna 62–3
Enoch 55–6, 61–3, 72
'enōsh (man) 78
Etemenanki 105
Euphrates 29
Eve 28, 47

faith, as communion with God 63
family tree
  of Adam 57–8, 59–63
  of Cain 54–7
  of Noah 98–104
  of Shem 108–12
  links with Mesopotamian tradition 61
flesh 38
flood story 4, 10–11, 64–87
  relationship to mythology 66
  Babylonian version 64
  Sumerian version 64

Genesis 1–11
  as prologue 8–9
  date of final written form 1–2
  duplicate narratives 4, 29
  religious teaching of 9, 107–8
  sources of 2–7
  transmission of 1–2
Gihon 32–3
Gilgamesh, epic of 29, 34–5, 39, 64–7, 81–2, 86
God
  concern for man 53–4, 80
  creative power of 16
  names of 3–4, 30, 58
  patience of 86
  sovereignty of 13–15
  transcendence of 14

Ham 94
Haran 111–12
Harran 110
heavenly court 24
hope 87, 92, 107

'ibrī (Hebrew) 104
image and likeness 24–5, 31
image of God 89
immortality
  man's search for 29, 34, 47
  as explanation of image of God 25
Irad (Jared) 55
Isaac 4
'īsh (man) 37
'ishshāh (woman) 37

'J' source 5–6, 28
Jabal 56
Japheth 63, 97
Javan 101
Jehovah 6
Jubal 56
judgement 43–6, 56, 80, 87
  aetiological element in 43

Kasdim 110–11
Kathar-Hasis 56
Kenites 50–1
Khnum 30
knowledge of good and evil 23–5, 40
kosher meat 88–9

Lamech 55–6
  sons of 57
life span
  abnormally high 61
  approaching normality 109–10
light 17
lights, stars and planets 21
LORD 4, 6

mabbul (flood) 75
man
  a living creature 30–1
  arrogance of 40
  expelled from Eden 46–8
  formed from the dust of the ground 30
  made in the image and likeness of God 24
  made in the likeness of God 62
  male and female 25–6
  sanctity of his life 89
  summary of teaching about 107
  temptation and disobedience of 39–41
  tragedy of 48, 87–9
  vegetarian 26
Marduk 13
Mari 110
Mehujael (Mahalalel) 55
Messiah 44
Methushael (Methuselah), 55, 61

Mot 11
Mizraim 102
myth 9–12
　aetiological element in 10–11, 43
　　50, 105
　and ritual 11–12
　creation myth 11–12
　Babylonian creation myth 13, 15
　cultural myth 94–5
　story myth 10, 28–9, 107

Nabopolassar 105
Nahor 111–12
name, significance of 37
nepesh (life) 31, 88
Nephilim 7, 69
New Year festival 13, 83
niham (bring...relief) 63
niham (sorry) 71
Nimrod 102–3
Noah 4, 71–97
　and the ark 74–5
　character of 72, 75, 76
　drunkenness of 94
　explanation of name 63
　God's covenant with 75, 91–3
　object of the LORD's favour 71
　offers sacrifice 85–6
　sends forth birds 82
　sons of 63, 94–7, 100
Nod 54
Nuzi 110, 111

oral tradition
　character of 5
　tenacity of 1
'*ōt* (sign) 91–2

'P' source 5–7, 14
Peleg 103–4
Pentateuch 3
Philistines 103
Pishon 32, 33
polygamy 56

rainbow, as sign of the covenant
　92
Rebecca 4

religion
　and astrology 21
　Canaanite 14–15, 26, 35
　ritual, myth and 11–12
rōbēts (demon) 52
Rodanim 102

sabbath 27
sacrifice 50–1, 85–6
　clean and unclean animals in 4,
　　47
Satan 39
sea-monster 22
serpent
　conflict with man 44
　nature of 39
　symbolic of evil 44
Seth 57–8
sex, attitude to in creation hymn
　25–6
sexual element in judgement 44–5
Shem 63, 95, 96
Sheol 53
Shinar 103, 105–7
sons of the gods 7, 69
spirit of God 16

Tabernacles, feast of 13
Tarshish 101
tehōm (abyss) 15
temptation 39–40
Terah 111–12
Tiamat 13–16
Tigris 29
TORAH (law) 3
tradition, transmission of 1–7
tree of the knowledge of good and
　evil 33–4
tree of life 29, 33–4, 47
tribal marks 50–1
tselem (image) 24–5
Tubal-cain 56

Ugarit 11
Ur 110–11
Utnapishtim 64–7

vault of heaven 18

waters
  divided by vault 18
  of chaos 15–16, 22
whole-offerings 85–6
wife–sister motif 4
wind (spirit) 16, 80
woman
  judgement on 44–5
  partner for man 37
  temptation of 40

word of God 17

YHWH (Yahweh)
  explanation of form 5–6
  name first used in worship 58

ziggurat 105
Ziusudra 64